Boundaries, Walls and Fences

Ninth Edition

Trevor M Aldridge
QC (Hon), MA (Cantab), Solicitor

LONDON
SWEET & MAXWELL
2004

First Published 1962
Ninth edition 2004

Published in 2004 by
Sweet & Maxwell Ltd, 100 Avenue Road
Swiss Cottage, London NW3 3PF
http://www.sweetandmaxwell.co.uk

Typeset by J&L Composition
Printed in Great Britain by TJ International Ltd, Padstow, Cornwall

No natural forests were destroyed to make this product;
only farmed timber was used and replanted.

A CIP catalogue record for this book is available from the
British Library

ISBN 0 421 859 105

AUSTRALIA
Law Book Co.
Sydney

CANADA and USA
Carswell
Toronto

HONG KONG
Sweet & Maxwell Asia

NEW ZEALAND
Brookers
Auckland

SINGAPORE and MALAYSIA
Sweet & Maxwell Asia
Singapore and Kuala Lumpur

Contents

4 Party Walls 45
  1 What is a party wall? 45
  2 Repairing party walls: overview 47
  3 Party Wall etc. Act 1996 47
  4 Common law obligations 56
  5 Other shared structures 59

5 Hedges 61
  1 Residential property 61
  2 Non-residential property 64
  3 Specific cases 65

6 Duty to Fence 67
  1 No general duty 67
  2 Obligations on freehold owners 67
  3 Landlord and tenant 70
  4 Fencing easements 73
  5 Obligations arising from particular circumstances 74
  6 Statutory obligations 79
  7 Obligation not to fence 80

7 Rights of Entry 81
  1 Common law position 81
  2 Statutory rights 82
  3 Access to Neighbouring Land Act 1992 83

8 Miscellaneous 89
  1 Planning 89
  2 Settled land 90
  3 Trusts of land 91
  4 Churchyards 91

Appendices 93
Appendix 1: Statutes 93
  Law of Property Act 1925 93
  Access to Neighbouring Land Act 1992 93
  Party Wall etc. Act 1996 105
  Land Registration Act 2002 126
  Anti-social Behaviour Act 2003 127
Appendix 2: Statutory Instruments 147
  Town & Country Planning (General Permitted
    Development) Order 1995 147
  Hedgerows Regulations 1997 148
  Land Registration Rules 2003 169

Index 173

Table of Cases

xii   TABLE OF CASES

Great Torrington Commons Conservators v Moore Stevens [1904] 1
  Ch. 347, Ch. D. 1–21
Grigsby v Melville [1974] 1 W.L.R. 80; [1973] 3 All E.R. 455; 26 P. &
  C.R. 182; 117 S.J. 632, CA 1–03, 1–20
Grosvenor Mayfair Estates, Re [1995] 2 E.G.L.R. 202; [1995] 38 E.G.
  142, Lands Tr 7–20
Habib Bank Ltd v Habib Bank AG [1981] 1 W.L.R. 1265; [1981] 2 All
  E.R. 650; [1982] R.P.C. 1; 125 S.J. 512, CA 3–02
Haines v Florensa (1990) 22 H.L.R. 238; (1990) 59 P. & C.R. 200;
  [1990] 09 E.G. 70, CA 1–38
Hale v Norfolk CC [2001] Ch. 717; [2001] 2 W.L.R. 1481; [2001]
  R.T.R. 26; [2001] J.P.L. 1093; [2000] E.G.C.S. 137; (2001) 98(2)
  L.S.G. 40; (2000) 144 S.J.L.B. 289; [2000] N.P.C. 122, The Times,
  December 19, 2000; Independent, November 22, 2000, CA 1–17
Hall v Dorling [1996] E.G.C.S. 58; [1996] N.P.C. 55, CA 1–16
Hall v Duke of Norfolk [1900] 2 Ch. 493, Ch. D. 4–22
Halsall v Brizell [1957] Ch. 169; [1957] 2 W.L.R. 123; [1957] 1 All E.R.
  371; 101 S.J. 88, Ch. D. 6–03
Harlow Development Corporation v Myers [1979] 1 E.G.L.R. 143;
  (1979) 249 E.G. 243, CC 6–26
Harrold v Watney [1898] 2 Q.B. 320, CA 6–01, 6–15
Hatfield v Moss [1988] 40 E.G. 112, CA 1–09, 1–38
Hatt & Co. (Bath) v Pearce [1978] 1 W.L.R. 885; [1978] 2 All E.R. 474;
  122 S.J. 180, CA 3–01
Haynes v Brassington [1988] E.G.C.S. 100 1–25
Henniker v Howard (1904) 90 L.T. 157, DC. 3–16
Hereford and Worcester CC v Newman; Worcestershire CC v Newar
  [1975] 1 W.L.R. 901; [1975] 2 All E.R. 673; 73 L.G.R. 461; 30 P. &
  C.R. 381; 119 S.J. 354, CA; affirming [1974] 1 W.L.R. 938, Q.B.D. . . 6–15
Hesketh v Willis Cruisers (1968) 19 P. & C.R. 573, CA 1–21
Highway Board of Macclesfield v Grant (1882) 51 L.J.Q.B. 357 4–23
Hilder v Associated Portland Cement Manufacturers Ltd [1961] 1
  W.L.R. 1434; [1961] 3 All E.R. 709; 105 S.J. 725, Q.B.D. 6–20
Hilton v Ankesson [1872] All E.R. Rep. 994, Ex Ct 6–12
Holgate v Bleazard [1917] 1 K.B. 443, KBD 6–19
Holland School v Wassef [2001] 2 E.G.L.R. 88; [2001] 29 E.G. 123,
  CC (Central London) 4–08
Hopgood v Brown [1955] 1 W.L.R. 213; [1955] 1 All E.R. 550; 99 S.J.
  168, CA 1–46
Hopwood v Cannock Chase; sub nom. Hopwood v Rugeley Urban
  DC [1975] 1 W.L.R. 373; [1975] 1 All E.R. 796; (1984) 13 H.L.R. 31;
  73 L.G.R. 137; (1975) 29 P. & C.R. 256; 119 S.J. 186, The Times,
  December 14, 1974, CA 6–09
Hoskin v Rogers (1985) 82 L.S.G. 848, CA 6–19
Hudson v Tabor (1876–77) L.R. 2 Q.B.D. 290, CA 6–12
Hull and Selby Railway, Re (1839) 5 M. & W. 327 . . . . 1–31, 1–49
Hunt v Harris (1855) 19 C.B. (N.S.) 13; New Report 63; 34 L.J.C.P. 249 . . 4–08
Ilkiw v Samuels [1963] 1 W.L.R. 991; [1963] 2 All E.R. 879; 107 S.J.
  680, CA 3–01

Table of Statutes

References in bold type are to the paragraph at which that Act is set out in full.

Table of Statutory Instruments

References References in bold type are to the paragraph at which that Statutory Instrument is set out in full.

Introduction

Boundaries are notorious troublemakers
Lloyd v Stanbury [1971] 1 W.L.R. 535, 542 *per* Brightman J.

O wall, O sweet, O lovely wall,
That standest between her father's ground and mine
A Midsummer Night's Dream, William Shakespeare

Good fences make good neighbours
North of Boston. Mending Wall, Robert Frost

Hedges have recently caused particular concern. The result has been two new sets of statutory rules, both dealt with in this new edition. The aims of the new rules seem contradictory: one is aimed at curbing troublesome hedges, which have grown too vigorously, the other at protecting hedges from removal.

The Anti-social Behaviour Act 2003 tackles the problem of high evergreen hedges, which can interfere with the reasonable enjoyment of domestic property. The Act allows the owner or occupier of property to complain to the local authority, which can direct that appropriate action be taken. On the other hand, hedgerows mainly in rural areas, and in any event not on or bordering residential property, are protected from removal. This applies to "important" hedges, which are generally those which are old or are valuable because of the wildlife they harbour or the species that make them up. Notice must be given to the local planning authority before starting any removal work and the authority may issue a notice to preserve the hedge.

A new chapter devoted to hedges gives details of both these procedures.

Boundaries continue to provoke disputes resulting in court decisions. Other developments in the law, such as changes to land registration, have affected the areas with which this book is concerned.

The contents have been extensively revised for this edition, so that it continues to provide a comprehensive yet handy guide to the law. The 2003 Act is treated as if it were in force; otherwise I have stated the law as at February 1, 2004.

Trevor M. Aldridge

Chapter 1

Determining Boundaries

1 Construing title deeds

(a) Parcels

Parcels of land in separate ownership may be divided horizontally, **1–01** vertically or in any other way (Law of Property Act (LPA) 1925, s.205(1)(ix)). As this power is unrestricted, the first consideration in determining boundaries is to look at the acts of the owners of the different parcels as revealed by the title deeds. A clear definition in the deeds will normally be conclusive. To this general rule there are a number of exceptions.

First, adverse occupation by a squatter for a sufficient time to acquire title under the Land Registration Act 2002 (for registered land) or under the Limitation Act 1980 (for unregistered land) may alter the boundary. Secondly, where a boundary of registered land is a non-tidal river or stream, a natural change of the stream's course will vary the boundary (Land Registration Act 2002, s.61(1)). Thirdly, an act of the landowner or one of his predecessors in title, although not varying the boundary shown on his deeds, may estop him from taking action in respect of the infringement. Fourthly, if the title deeds to the adjoining properties conflict, then reference will have to be made to the deeds showing the original division.

The limitation on the commencement of title to unregistered land in s.44 of the LPA 1925 (as amended by the LPA 1969, s.23), applies to matters between vendor and purchaser, and would not bar an older deed being adduced in evidence in a boundary dispute. Similarly, because of the general rule that Land Registry plans do not necessarily show precise boundaries, reference may need to be made in cases of registered title to pre-registration deeds.

Fifthly, a deed containing an error by both parties to it, or not accurately representing their prior agreement, will normally be rectified by the court, unless the applicant has disentitled himself to equitable relief, *e.g.* by laches. Sixthly, the boundary may subsequently be varied by statute, although evidence of this should have been placed with or indorsed upon the deeds.

(b) Ambiguity

1–02 If the definition of the parcels is clear, and yet some further erroneous description is added to it, the latter may be disregarded, applying the maxim *falsa demonstratio non nocet*. This applies where a deed defines boundaries by reference to existing physical objects, and also states the area of the land, and the two descriptions disagree. The description by physical objects will prevail. Thus, if a lease of land describes the premises by admeasurement and adds "with the houses now erected or being erected thereon" and the foundations have already been laid and extend beyond the boundaries according to the measurements, the description by measurements is disregarded and the boundaries extend to include the foundations (*Manning v Fitzgerald* (1859) 29 L.J. Ex. 24). The maxim applied in that case to reject the first description.

Another example of the application of the maxim is a case where land was described in a tabulated schedule to a conveyance. The second column, headed "description", referred to a plan that clearly showed an area conveyed of 27 perches. The fourth column of the schedule gave the area as 34 perches. The larger figure, coming second, was treated as erroneous and disregarded (*Llewellyn v Earl of Jersey* (1843) 11 M. & W. 183).

Should there be a number of conflicting descriptions, however, the maxim *falsa demonstratio non nocet* is not available to permit all but the first to be discarded. The order is not in that case paramount (*Eastwood v Ashton* [1915] A.C. 900). Which description prevails is a question of construction; there are no general presumptions. The description may be so muddled and inaccurate that it offers no assistance in determining the boundary, as *e.g.* where it referred to a 1932 Ordnance Survey plan when there was none that year but one dated 1933 and plot numbers were quoted from different editions of the map (*Affleck v Shorefield Holidays Ltd* [1997] E.G.C.S. 159). In that case, the words must be ignored.

It is sometimes possible to admit extrinsic evidence of the parties' intentions, *e.g.* that both landlord and tenant meant to include a rear storeroom when they only referred to a shop (*IS Mills (Yardley) Ltd v Curdworth Investments Ltd* [1975] 2 E.G.L.R. 54).

(c) Descriptive words

1–03 Certain words have acquired a technical meaning, and where they occur in a description of property they can assist in defining the boundaries. "Messuage" and "house" both pass a dwelling-house with its curtilage, attached garden and buildings appurtenant to it.

"Dwelling-house" is not limited to the part of the building that happens to be occupied for residential purposes (*Grigsby v Melville* [1974] 1 W.L.R. 80). "Curtilage" means land that belongs to a house in the physical sense. The term can be used for the land that goes with other buildings, *e.g.* a church (*Re St John's Church, Bishop's Hatfield* [1967] P. 113). Land is sometimes described as having a building erected on it "or on some part thereof". This implies that more than the mere site of the building is referred to (*Bisney v Swanston* (1973) 225 E.G. 2299).

"Farm" passes the farmhouse and the land held with it. "Water" passes the right to water and fishing, but not the land beneath it. "Pool" passes both the water and its bed.

Where it is clear that the intention of the deed is to convey the whole of the grantor's holding, evidence of the extent of that holding will be admitted to construe the deed (*Maxted v Plymouth Corporation* [1957] C.L.Y. 243). If all but a small part of the grantor's land is conveyed and no intention to retain any has been displayed (as where the title deeds are handed over), the whole plot with its original boundaries will be presumed to be conveyed, in the absence of contrary evidence.

The position of a fence may itself determine the interpretation in the context of a "close" or "curtilage" (*Walsh v Allweather Mechanical Grouting Co. Ltd* [1959] 2 Q.B. 300: not a case interpreting a title deed).

(d) General words

The general words implied into the description of the parcels in a **1–04** conveyance by s.62 of the LPA 1925 can extend the amount of property that appears to be conveyed, and therefore affects its boundary. In a case where the parcels were described in the deed and shown coloured on a plan, part of a yard that was not coloured was conveyed because one of the general words was "yard" and was held to include it (*Willis v Watney* (1881) 51 L.J. Ch. 588).

2 Plans

A plan referred to may be drawn on or annexed to the deed, form **1–05** part of another deed or be independent of the title, *e.g.* an Ordnance Survey or tithe map. If the plan is to be of assistance, it will have to be sufficiently clear and detailed to be self-explanatory.

(a) Ordnance Survey

Ordnance Survey practice, where there are boundary features such as **1–06** hedges or fences between parcels of land, is to draw the boundary

FIGURE 1.1

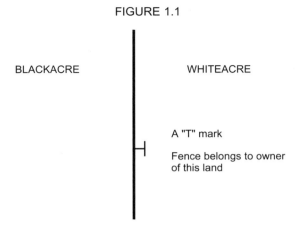

BLACKACRE

WHITEACRE

A "T" mark

Fence belongs to owner
of this land

line down the middle of these features. General presumptions, which may suggest that the boundary should lie down one side or the other, are ignored. This will apply to plans that do not explicitly state that they are extracts from, or based upon, the Ordnance Survey, but which can be seen to be so (*e.g.* because the Ordnance Survey parcel numbers are given).

(b) "T" and "H" marks

1–07   It is the practice to define the ownership of boundary features, or the responsibility for their maintenance, by inserting "T" marks. The convention is that the "T" is written, with its cross stroke parallel to the boundary and its down stroke touching it, on the side of the boundary on which lies the property with which the feature is included (see Figure 1.1). There is no authority to suggest that this is anything more than a convention.

If, as sometimes happens, "T" marks appear on the plan without any reference to them in the deed, they can be no more than persuasive evidence of the ownership of the boundary features. Since 1962 "T" marks have been shown on the filed plan of land with registered title in certain circumstances. This does not, however, invest them with any greater significance than they would have when considering the precise position of the boundary of unregistered land.

Occasionally, an "H" mark will be found, but much less frequently than "T" marks. The "H" is written so that its vertical strokes are parallel to the boundary, one on each side of it, so that it is, in effect, two "T" marks joined. This is intended to indicate a party wall (see Figure 1.2). Because of the ambiguity of that expression, and because "H" marks are not used frequently enough for a universal

FIGURE 1.2

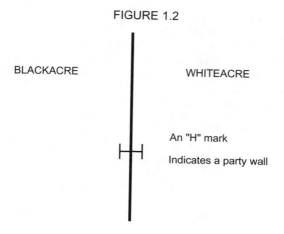

BLACKACRE

WHITEACRE

An "H" mark
Indicates a party wall

practice to have been established, they cannot be regarded as of any evidential value if they appear without any verbal explanation.

(c) Effect on parcels

An incomplete verbal description of premises in a deed may be supplemented by reference to any plan to which the deed refers. Indeed, it has been said "where parcels in a conveyancing document are described by reference to a plan attached to the document, the natural inference is that it was the intention that anyone concerned should see from the document alone, which means from the plan on it, what land the document was purporting to pass" (*AJ Dunning & Sons (Shopfitters) Ltd v Sykes & Son (Poole) Ltd* [1987] Ch. 287 at 299 *per* Dillon L.J.). Where the wording of the conveyance is ambiguous, a plan annexed to the conveyance, even if not referred to, may be considered (*Leachman v L & K Richardson Ltd* [1969] 1 W.L.R. 1129).

1–08

Should the verbal description of the parcels and the plan disagree, it is a question of construction of the deed's reference to the plan, to determine which will prevail. It may be possible to adduce extrinsic evidence (*Scarfe v Adams* [1981] 1 All E.R. 843). When the words are not clear, but go on to define the property as "more particularly described" on the plan, the latter will prevail (*Eastwood v Ashton* [1915] A.C. 900).

The plan may influence the construction of the words of the deed. A house described as "comprising that portion of Terrant Monkton House which was formerly known as the Old Rectory" was not restricted to what had been the Old Rectory when more was shown on the plan. "Comprising" was construed as "including" (*Smout v*

Farquharson (1973) 226 E.G. 114). Where there is no conflict between the description and the plan, even a plan for identification can supplement the verbal description (*Tebaldi v Wiseman and Kemp* (1983) 133 N.L.J. 1042: the plan on a lease of a basement flat showed that the internal staircase down to it was included in the demise).

The maxim *falsa demonstratio non nocet* can apply here also. Where the deed's description makes it clear that the boundary runs along the centre line of a hedge, but adds "which said piece of land is delineated on the plan drawn hereon" and the plan shows the boundary lines at the foot of the hedge, the plan is ignored and the boundary is in the middle of the hedge (*Maxted v Plymouth Corporation* [1957] C.L.Y. 243). On the other hand, if, as a matter of construction, the description of the property in the parcels of a conveyance is to be read as a whole, dimensions given in the verbal description can prevail over an inaccurate plan (*Boyd Gibbins Ltd v Hockham* (1966) 199 E.G. 229).

(d) For identification only

1–09   In principle, a plan that the deed states to be "for identification only" should be used to show the general location of the land, but not its precise extent (*Moreton C Cullimore (Gravels) Ltd v Routledge* (1977) 121 S.J. 202). Nevertheless, it can supplement a verbal description which is not clear (*Wiggington & Milner Ltd v Winster Engineering Ltd* [1978] 1 W.L.R. 1462; *Hatfield v Moss* [1988] 2 E.G.L.R. 58) or does not answer all the problems (*Targett v Ferguson* (1996) 72 P. & C.R. 106). The surrounding physical circumstances can also be taken into account where it is necessary to resort to a plan expressed to be for identification only, *e.g.* the position of a boundary pegged out on the ground (*Willson v Greene* [1971] 1 W.L.R. 635).

A plan "for identification only" is not acceptable for Land Registry purposes. Nevertheless, there are in fact many registered leases – which, unlike transfers, do not have to be in a prescribed form – with plans referred to in this way.

A plan stated to be "for the purposes of delineation only" is one not true to scale (*Re Freeman and Taylor's Contract* (1907) 97 L.T. 39).

3 Presumptions in certain cases

1–10   Where the boundaries of land are defined by reference to, or in fact follow, certain physical features, advantage may be taken of legal presumptions applicable to land bounded by such features, which will apply unless or until rebutted by contrary evidence (*Beaufort (Duke) v Swansea Corporation* (1849) 3 Exch. 413). In one case, a plan prepared for an auction some 75 years earlier provided such contrary evidence (*Falkingham v Farley* (1991) *The Times*, March 11). It must be emphasised that these presumptions may be modified or excluded where the title to the land is registered. Assistance may also be gained from statutory rules where the adjoining property is used for certain purposes. Listed alphabetically below are a number of features by which boundaries may be defined, with particulars of whether, and if so, what special rules apply in each case.

(a) Beach
"Beach" is not a term of art. When used to define a boundary it may   **1–11**
prima facie have the same meaning as "seashore" (*Government of State of Penang v Beng Hong Oon* [1972] A.C. 425). However, it can extend further – to include land in apparent continuity with the beach at high water mark, *i.e.* until there is a change of vegetation, a physical barrier, or a road (*Tito v Waddell (No.2)* [1977] Ch. 106, 263).

(b) Canals
Artificial waterways are not subject to the presumptions noted below   **1–12**
in respect of certain rivers, where the riparian lands extend to the centre of the stream, because they must have been originally dug by a person on his own land or on land acquired from the adjoining owners for the purpose. Land bordering a canal is bounded by it, so minerals beneath the canal do not pass on a conveyance of the bordering land that does not expressly include the canal, or some part of it, even though they belong to the transferor (*Chamber Colliery Co. v Rochdale Canal Co.* [1895] A.C. 564).

(c) Flats
A part of a house, divided horizontally or vertically, which is leased   **1–13**
separately includes the external walls enclosing that part, unless there are provisions to the contrary in the lease. A covenant by the landlord to do external repairs is not sufficient to displace this presumption (*Sturge v Hackett* [1962] 1 W.L.R. 1257). The outside of a flat can be expressly excluded from a demise of it, but that does not prevent the external walls from constituting its exterior for the purposes of the landlord's implied repairing obligations (*Campden Hill Towers Ltd v Gardner* [1977] Q.B. 823).

(d) Foreshore
See *(q) Seashore*, below.   **1–14**

(e) Forests
The boundaries of the royal forests – most of which are vested in   **1–15**
the Secretary of State for the Environment, Food and Rural Affairs and managed by the Forestry Commission – were finally fixed, after

considerable friction between the Crown and its subjects, by the Delimitation of Forests Act 1640. This necessarily also fixed the boundaries of the private lands adjoining the forests. Since then, however, considerable areas have been disafforested by special statutes, private inclosure acts, and letters patent. These have mostly passed into private ownership.

FIGURE 1.3

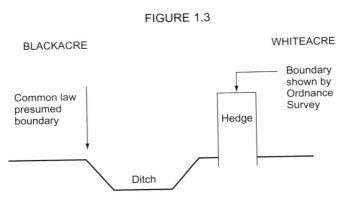

(f) *Hedges and ditches*

1–16   Where two fields are separated by an artificial ditch alongside a bank, with or without a hedge or fence on it, there is a presumption that the boundary is along the edge of the ditch furthest from the bank (*Fisher v Winch* [1939] 1 K.B. 666) (see Figure 1.3). But "the presumption only comes into operation in cases where the boundary is not delimited in the parcels to the conveyance" (at 673 *per* Lord Greene M.R.). This is because it is assumed that the landowner digs his drainage ditch on the extreme edge of his property and throws up the earth on to his own side of the ditch to avoid committing a trespass against his neighbour.* This forms the bank upon which he plants a hedge or erects a fence (*Vowles v Miller* (1810) 3 Taunt. 137, 138 *per* Lawrence J.). The presumption only applies to a single hedge (or fence or bank) and ditch. If there is one without the other, or two hedges or two ditches, no such presumption operates, because the original landowner's actions in digging the ditch or planting the hedge cannot be logically deduced. Similarly, because the presumption is based on a landowner's action in digging the ditch, it probably does not apply where the ditch is natural and not artificial (*Marshall v Taylor* [1895] 1 Ch. 641, 647).

---

* According to a correspondent to *The Times* in 1999, the presumption only applies for certain to "statutory hedges", bounding areas of land allocated under an inclosure award.

Although this is only a presumption, a conveyance that purports to convey land that did not belong to the seller does not displace it (*Hall v Dorling* (1996) 74 P. & C.R. 401).

Ordnance Survey practice is to take the centre line of the hedge as the boundary (see Figure 1.3). Judicial notice of this practice has been taken in a consistory court (*Re St Peter and St Paul, Scrayingham* [1992] 1 W.L.R. 187). Whether or not the Ordnance Survey practice overrides the common law presumption depends on the circumstances. Where land had been consistently conveyed by reference to Ordnance Survey plans, the centre of the hedge was the boundary (*Davey v Harrow Corporation* [1958] 1 Q.B. 60). However, in the case of two pieces of land that had never been in common ownership, one of which was conveyed by reference to an Ordnance Survey plan "for identification only", the common law presumption prevailed (*Alan Wibberley Building Ltd v Insley* [1999] 1 W.L.R. 894).

(g) Highways

If a highway is fenced on both sides, it will be presumed to extend up   **1–17**
to both fences (or hedges). But this only applies if it can be shown that the fences were erected (or hedges planted) to separate the adjoining closes from the highway (*Attorney-General v Beynon* [1970] Ch. 1). The presumption extends to land between other boundary features, *e.g.* banks, whether natural or man-made (*Naydler v Hampshire County Council* (1973) 226 E.G. 176). This, however, is no more than a presumption. It may be rebutted, *e.g.* if it is established that the fence pre-dated the highway (*Minting v Ramage* [1991] E.G.C.S. 12) or if the facts show that the owner had no intention of dedicating the relevant land (*Hale v Norfolk County Council* [2001] Ch. 717).

There are said to be two occasions on which a presumption arises as to the boundary of land adjoining a highway. First, the boundary of land adjoining a highway is presumed to be a line drawn down the middle of the highway, and land "adjoins" a highway for this purpose although separated from it by a public right of way not being part of the street (*Ware Urban District Council v Gaunt* [1960] 1 W.L.R. 1364). This presumption only applies where the conveyancing history of the land and the road is unknown (*Giles v County Building Constructors (Hertford) Ltd* (1971) 22 P. & C.R. 978, 981).

For the purpose of making up and adopting private roads, road charges are normally imposed on the owners of the property "fronting" (which includes "adjoining": Highways Act 1980, s.203(3)) the street (s.205). An upper maisonette, separated from the highway by a 25 foot garden belonging to the lower maisonette, does not adjoin the highway for this purpose (*Buckinghamshire County Council v Trigg* [1963] 1 W.L.R. 155). But leaving a 12 foot strip of land between a housing development and the road, to accommodate future widening, does not prevent the houses fronting the road (*Warwickshire County Council v Adkins* (1967) 112 S.J. 135).

1–18   The second case in which there may be a presumption is on the conveyance of land forming part of a building estate. It can include half the road, even though it clearly describes the property as excluding any part of the road. Very little now seems to be needed to rebut this presumption (*Giles v County Building Constructors (Hertford) Ltd* (1971) 22 P. & C.R. 978).

The surface of that part of the land comprising the highway is not normally vested in the adjoining owner, but the boundary is important in passing the ground beneath the surface with its minerals and possible basement accommodation. In such a case, the ownership of growing trees remains in the owner of the subsoil, although the management and control of them may be assumed by the highway authority (*Russell v London Borough of Barnet* [1984] 2 E.G.L.R. 44).

The boundary also needs to be considered where a stopping-up order is obtained so that the surface reverts to private ownership. In some cases where the land was conveyed to the highway authority (not dedicated), a stopping-up order will only extinguish the public rights over the surface, the land remaining vested in the highway authority. The boundaries are then unaffected. Where only part of a highway is affected by a stopping-up order it is thought that this does not affect the position of the boundary, which thereafter need not be in the centre of the remaining road. The boundary is fixed on the first conveyance of the land, and all that is changed are the rights that may be exercised over part of the surface of the plot. Where it is not practicable to trace the original conveyance, such evidence of the facts as is available will have to be relied upon. Statutory declarations as to the practice in the past made by independent persons would normally be accepted in a conveyancing transaction; evidence admissible in court is considered below.

1–19   In the case of registered land the half of the highway is excluded from the registration of the title of the adjoining land if adopted by the local authority. This was started as an application of the general boundaries rule, and applied even in cases of an express conveyance of half the roadway. However, it is now clear that where the highway authority has the surface vested in it, it acquires a legal estate (*Tithe Redemption Commission v Runcorn Urban District Council* [1954] Ch. 383), so it would not be proper to do otherwise. The presumption still applies to the subsoil.

The presumption of ownership of half an adjoining highway is displaced by evidence showing an intention not to include any part of the road. In one case, the presumption did not apply where a sewer was to be laid under the road by the authority leasing the adjoining land, and there was even doubt whether they had power to include it (*Mappin Brothers v Liberty & Co. Ltd* [1903] 1 Ch. 118).

A dispute about the boundary of a highway may be settled by the application of the general law about what can constitute a highway. In one case the question arose whether a stone buttress built on private land at the edge of a public highway that had no verge could have been dedicated, which would have moved the boundary. The possibility was ruled out, because the land in question could not be used for a right of passage as would be required for a highway (*Skrenty v Harrogate Borough Council* [1999] E.G.C.S. 127).

(h) Houses

Where a house is conveyed or demised there is a presumption that it passes in its entirety, including projecting eaves and footings (although not shown on the plan referred to), but not the air space between them (*Truckell v Stock* [1957] 1 W.L.R. 161). On the other hand, a conveyance of property by reference to the ground plan of a building will include part of a neighbouring building which over-hangs above it (*Laybourn v Gridley* [1892] 2 Ch. 53). A conveyance of a dwelling-house by description passed with it a void under the ground floor, even though the only access to that basement was from the adjoining property, with which it had previously been enjoyed (*Grigsby v Melville* [1974] 1 W.L.R. 80).   **1–20**

Walls that are shared by two properties (*e.g.* those between semi-detached or terraced houses) may belong to one of the adjoining houses exclusively if there is clear evidence that the wall is on one side of the boundary line. It is usual, however, for them to be party walls, and in the absence of contrary evidence there is a presumption that the boundary runs down the middle of the wall.

Where land is conveyed described as bounded by a house, or something else to which title would normally be made independently, the boundary object is completely excluded.

(i) Islands

Ownership of the bank of a non-tidal river does not carry with it islands up to a line midway between the two banks. The riparian owner's boundary is in the middle of the stream between the bank and the island (*Great Torrington Commons Conservators v Moore Stevens* [1904] 1 Ch. 347). There is no settled presumption, however, on the line of the boundary round the ends of the island facing up and down stream (see Figure 1.4).   **1–21**

The boundary of an island is similarly in the middle of the stream. If the title to the island is registered, with the boundary shown at the water's edge, the presumption applies. It is not displaced by a claim to a corporeal fishery over more than half the stream, because being

FIGURE 1.4

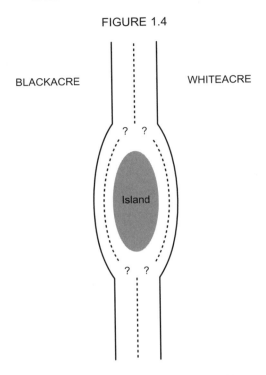

BLACKACRE   WHITEACRE

Two banks of river and an island, each in separate ownership.

By presumption, the boundary lies midstream between the two river banks, or the bank and the island.

How the boundary runs at the end of the island is unclear.

land it would itself have to be registered (*Hesketh v Willis Cruisers Ltd* (1968) 19 P. & C.R. 573).

The position is different when islands are formed by the water suddenly cutting off what was formerly part of the bank, or laying bare land formerly covered by water. Those islands belong to the riparian owners, the boundary being drawn where it was before the islands were formed. In tidal rivers, islands created by uncovering the river bed (even if only at low tide), or to which the riparian owners or some other person cannot make title, belong to the Crown. If part of a riparian owner's land is suddenly cut off by the waters of a tidal river, his boundary remains unaltered and extends round the island.

There are no presumptions relating to islands in lakes.

(j) Lakes

There is no settled presumption about the position of the boundary   **1–22**
between properties in different ownership separated by a lake. The
question of whether a rule similar to that for rivers applies, was left
undecided in a nineteenth century case (*Marshall v Ulleswater Steam
Navigation Company* (1863) L.R. 7 Q.B. 166). Evidence of exclusive
possession will normally be conclusive. A lake wholly within the
boundaries of a parcel of land will pass without special reference,
unless expressly excluded. Equally, a lake could be conveyed separately from any surrounding property, when its boundaries, if not
defined, would probably be the water's edge at the normal water
level.

Where land adjoining a lake is conveyed, the lake forms its boundary. Gradual accretions to the land, as a result of natural forces,
become part of it. The boundary moves to the position of the edge
of the lake for the time being (*Southern Centre of Theosophy Inc. v
State of South Australia* [1982] A.C. 706). Presumably, the same
applies, in reverse, if the lake shore is eroded. This rule now has
statutory force for registered land (Land Registration Act 2002,
s.61(1)).

(k) Pipe-lines

The grant of an easement for a pipe or wire may give exclusive rights   **1–23**
of use. The boundaries of the land over which the easement is
granted do not extend beyond the physical extent of the pipe, etc.,
unless otherwise stated, but such an easement will automatically
carry ancillary rights of entry for inspection, cleaning, repair and
replacement (*Jones v Pritchard* [1908] 1 Ch. 630). Land through
which passes a pipeline authorised by the Pipelines Act 1962 may
have been acquired by the pipe-line owner, or he may only have
rights of user. A plan showing the route and extent of a pipe-line
authorised to be laid or diverted under the Act must be deposited
with the local authorities of the areas affected (s.35). This plan is
open for inspection by anyone at all reasonable times without fee.

(l) Railways

No special presumption applies to railways. The boundary is where   **1–24**
it appears to be and not in the centre of the track, because the land
on which the railway is built had to be acquired from the adjoining
owner and became a separate plot at that date. Adjoining landowners are therefore not automatically entitled to minerals under the
railway (*Thompson v Hickman* [1907] 1 Ch. 550). However, conveyances under the Railways Clauses Consolidation Act 1845, s.77,
do not pass the mines and minerals unless expressly included, and
they therefore remain vested in the grantor who may well be the

adjoining owner. This section is taken to apply to Land Registry transfers where appropriate.
The boundary of a railway will usually be such as to include the boundary fence with the railway, by reason of the fencing obligations imposed on railway companies by the Railways Clauses Consolidation Act 1845, s.68. These obligations may not, however, apply.

(m) Rights of way

1–25   Where a private right of way forms a boundary, the same presumption arises as for highways, *i.e.* the centre line of the path or roadway is the boundary (*Lang v House* (1961) 178 E.G. 801). But in this case the land up to the half-way line remains vested in the adjoining owners (subject only to the rights of way), and will not be excluded from a registered title. The extent of the right of way itself may depend on the use to which it is put. A reservation that included the passage of cattle extended beyond the metalled road to include the verges (*Haynes v Brassington* [1988] E.G.C.S. 100).

(n) Rivers

1–26   In the case of non-tidal rivers, the boundary of the riparian lands is presumed to be in the centre of the stream. This presumption extends to the river Tweed where it forms the boundary between England and Scotland (*Lovett v Fairclough* (1990) 61 P. & C.R. 385).

. . . Where land adjoining . . . [an] inland river is granted, the *prima facie* presumption is, that the parties intended to include in the grant a moiety . . . of the river bed . . . ; and that such general presumption ought to prevail, unless there is something to indicate a contrary intention (*Dwyer v Rich* (1871) Ir. Rep. 6 Ch. 144, 149).

A contrary intention may be shown by one riparian owner performing acts of ownership. This was so in one case where he exercised them lower down the stream at a point where the other bank was a third party's property (*Jones v Williams* (1837) 2 M. & W. 326).
The presumption applies not only on the conveyance of freehold land bounded by a river, but also on the grant of a lease of such land (*Tilbury v Silva* (1890) 45 Ch. D. 98, 109 *per* Kay J.). The same rule applies to the limits of riparian owners' fishing rights in Scotland (*Fothringham v Kerr* (1984) 48 P. & C.R. 173). The presumption is not displaced by the fact that the grantor owns both banks of the river nor by facts, which only came to light later that, had they been known, might have induced him to reserve the river bed (*Micklethwait v Newlay Bridge Co.* (1886) 23 Ch. D. 133).

1–27   When the river and the adjoining bank are each conveyed separately without the boundary being defined, the division is at the water's edge (*Bridden v Fenn* [1986] C.L.Y. 2830 (CC)). If there is evidence that the river and its bed belong to some person other than the riparian owners, this rebuts the presumption. The boundary is the water line when the river is in its natural state, disregarding seasonal fluctuations. Evidence of independent ownership would be either normal conveyancing evidence of title, long possession as of right, or acts of ownership (*Jones v Williams* (1837) 2 M. & W. 326).

If there are gradual, imperceptible accretions to either bank in the ordinary course of nature, the additional land belongs to that riparian owner and the boundary in the centre of the stream is automatically adjusted, even though the original boundary may still be ascertainable (*Foster v Wright* (1878) 4 C.P.D. 438). If, however, the river suddenly completely changes its course, the boundary remains where it was immediately before the diversion (*Ford v Lacy* (1861) 7 H. & N. 151). When two riparian owners in Scotland agreed to divert the river defining their boundary, the result was to draw the boundary along the new course of the river (*Stirling v Bartlett* (1992) *The Times*, October 29).

The soil of the bed of a river where it is tidal *prima facie* belongs to the Crown (being managed by the Crown Estate Commissioners (Coast Protection Act 1949), except in the cases of the rivers Thames and Tees). It continues to do so even if the river gradually changes course (*Carlisle Corporation v Graham* (1869) L.R. 4 Ex. 361). The boundary on each side is medium high water. Accordingly, the fishing on such stretches of river does not pass with the riparian lands, as it normally does on non-tidal waters.

(o) Roads
See *(g) Highways*, above.   **1–28**

(p) Rooms
Where a room is demised without any precise definition of its   **1–29**
boundaries, the position varies according to whether its walls constitute outside walls of the building, or partition walls. The whole of any outside wall is included, but only an undefined part of a partition wall passes with the room (*Phelps v City of London Corporation* [1916] 2 Ch. 255, 263).

(q) Seashore
The technical name for the seashore is "foreshore", but in an appro-   **1–30**
priate context, where this is meant, these words are synonymous (*Mellor v Walmesley* [1905] 2 Ch. 164). The boundary between the seashore and the adjoining land is presumed to be the line of medium high tide between the ordinary spring and neap tides (*Attorney-General v Chambers* (1854) 4 De G.M. & G. 206). The

lower boundary of the seashore is the medium low water mark. In Scotland, the rule is that the boundary lies at the high water mark of the ordinary spring tides (*Mussleburgh Real Estate Co. Ltd v Mussleburgh Provost* [1905] A.C. 491).

Nevertheless, if the evidence warrants, "foreshore" can mean the whole of the shore from time to time exposed by the receding tide: the ordinary, everyday connotation of the word (*Loose v Castleton* (1978) 41 P. & C.R. 19, 34 *per* Bridge L.J.).

The "low water line" is necessarily one which moves with the seasons. ". . . there is no established rule of law that the low water mark is necessarily the line of median low water, and the principle which identifies the landwards boundary of the foreshore at the line of median high water depends on factors which have no application to the seaward low water mark. Nor is there any general rule as to the meaning of 'low water line' or 'low water mark'" (*Anderson v Alnwick District Council* [1993] 1 W.L.R. 1156 at 1165 *per* Evans L.J.).

1–31   A conveyance of land described as bounded by the seashore, but containing measurements making it clear that there is a strip of land between that conveyed and the seashore, estops the grantor denying the grantee access to the seashore over that strip, but does not convey the strip (*Mellor v Walmesley* [1905] 2 Ch. 164). If the medium high tide line moves, the boundary of land described as bounded by the seashore moves with it. This is a moveable freehold (*Scratton v Brown* (1825) 4 B. & C. 485; *Smart & Co. v Suva Town Board* [1893] A.C. 301). This is the effect of imperceptible accretions to the shore, that add to the land in private ownership, or of gradual erosion which returns land to the ownership of the Crown (*Re Hull and Selby Railway* (1839) 5 M. & W. 139). The common law treats the land as if it had always, since the limit of legal memory, been as it now is (*Mercer v Denne* [1905] 2 Ch. 538).

Whether land conveyed is in fact bounded by a moveable line, or whether the boundary is fixed in the place to which the tide came when the deed was executed, is a question of construction of the document (*Baxendale v Instow Parish Council* [1982] Ch. 14). The fact that there are physical markers showing the boundary line in its original position does not necessarily prevent the boundary being altered by natural forces (*Attorney-General v M'Carthy* [1911] 2 I.R. 260).

Land reclaimed by the owner of land bounded by the sea does not belong to him, but to the Crown (*Attorney-General of Southern Nigeria v John Holt and Company (Liverpool) Ltd* [1915] A.C. 599).

(r) Waste land

1–32   Where a fenced close adjoins waste land, there is a presumption that the fence belongs to the owner of the close (*White v Taylor (No.2)* [1960] 1 Ch. 160).

4 Other evidence of boundaries

Other forms of evidence of the position of boundaries may be avail-   **1–33**
able. These are discussed in relation to boundary disputes, where
their admissibility in accordance with the strict rules of evidence is
considered.

5 Horizontal boundaries

(a) Minerals
Although mines and minerals are readily severable from the surface   **1–34**
of the land, there is normally no definition of the boundary between
them and the surface. It would appear that the owner of the minerals can work any substance which comes within the definition of
minerals and to which he is entitled (not *e.g.* coal), so long as it is
below the surface. It may be noted that certain conveyances (including Land Registry transfers) exclude mines and minerals unless they
are expressly included (under the Railways Clauses Consolidation
Act 1845, s.77, and the Waterworks Clauses Act 1847, s.18).

(b) Highways
The rights of the public to use a highway extend only to the surface   **1–35**
of it. "'Street' . . . includes the surface and so much of the depth as
may be not unfairly used, as streets are used" (*Coverdale v Charlton*
(1878) 4 Q.B.D. 104, 121, *per* Brett L.J.). Or, as it was put earlier, ". . .
the King has nothing but the passage for himself and his people:
but the freehold and all profits belong to the owner of the soil. So do
all the trees upon it, and mines under it . . ." (*Goodtitle v Alker* (1757)
1 Burr. 133, 143 *per* Lord Mansfield). This defines the extent of the
property of which the highway authority can make use. Those rights
do not permit the use for other amenities, such as underground public conveniences, even though constructed by the highway authority
(*Tunbridge Wells Corporation v Baird* [1896] A.C. 434). Statute may,
however, confer rights on the highway or other authorities to construct under highways these and other amenities (*e.g.* car parks),
which the common law would not permit. The highway authority
has a legal estate in so much of the surface land as is vested in it for
highway purposes. This is a determinable fee simple, lasting only
while the use as a highway continues (*Tithe Redemption Commission
v Runcorn Urban District Council* [1954] Ch. 383).

(c) Streams
Although running water is not capable of being owned, a stream   **1–36**
may be vested in a different person from its bed. A stream may *e.g.*

be a public sewer, and so vested in a water company as successor to the water authority (Public Health Act 1936, s.20; Water Act 1973, Sch.8, para.33; repealed), while the bed remains the property of the riparian owners. The boundary between the bed and the stream above it is not subject to any legal presumption, but must be the place at which the liquid of the stream physically meets the solid substance of the bed.

(d) Basements

1–37 Basements of premises adjoining streets built lying under the street can extend up to the horizontal boundary between the highway and the subsoil. Where the basement has existed for some time this will be excellent evidence of the lowest possible limit of the surface in cases where the highway authority later wishes to extend its occupation downwards. Although roads adopted by the local authority are excluded from registered titles, basements under them will be included in the registration if the position is made clear to the Land Registry.

(e) Flats and maisonettes

1–38 There are no settled presumptions determining the horizontal boundary of a flat (or maisonette) from the one above or below it. However, "it is the general expectation of anyone who takes the lease of a flat that he acquires the space between the floor of his flat and the underneath of the floor of the flat above" (*Graystone Property Investments Ltd v Margulies* (1983) 47 P. & C.R. 472, 474, *per* Griffiths L.J.).

The terms of the lease demising the property may, by implication, help to decide the point. So, an express demise of the roof carried with it the air above (*Davies v Yadegar* [1990] 1 E.G.L.R. 70). The same applied where there was an express restriction on improvements carried out there (*Haines v Florensa* [1990] 1 E.G.L.R. 73) and the roof was included in the demise where there was an express obligation to repair it (*Straudley Investments Ltd v Barpress Ltd* [1987] 1 E.G.L.R. 69).

The Court of Appeal has accepted that the upper boundary is not lower than the underside of the floor joists to which the ceiling is fixed, but it left undecided the question whether in fact the flat extends upwards to half-way through the joists, or even to the upperside of them (*Sturge v Hackett* [1962] 1 W.L.R. 1257, 1266). In particular circumstances, a flat included a void created by false suspended ceilings which were lower than the original ceilings (*Graystone Property Investments Ltd v Margulies*, above). The demise of a top floor flat may, but does not necessarily, include the roof space above it (*Hatfield v Moss* [1988] 2 E.G.L.R. 58) and even the roof. Whether it does is a matter of construction of the document (*Cockburn v Smith* [1924] 2 K.B. 119).

Where the lower boundary is not defined, at least some part of the floor is included (*Phelps v City of London Corporation* [1916] 2 Ch. 255, 264). The divisions are sometimes referred to as "party floors" or "party ceilings". In the case of party walls there is a presumption in the absence of contrary evidence that the boundary runs down the middle, but it is doubtful whether this applies to floors and ceilings. Some of the provisions of the Party Wall etc. Act 1996 may apply. But the provisions of the LPA 1925, s.38, do not; they do not envisage hollow structures which most floors and ceilings are, and they only deal with a vertical division.

(f) Building with air beneath
In the unusual case of a building suspended over air in separate   **1–39**
ownership – *e.g.* a first floor building with an open passage way underneath – the whole of the building's lower wall, including brick vaulting, belongs to the owner of the building (*Cresswell v Duke of Westminster* [1985] 2 E.G.L.R. 151).

6 Registered land

(a) General boundaries
Originally, all the boundaries of registered land had to be precisely   **1–40**
defined (Land Registry Act 1862, ss.10, 16, 25(3)). That was found to be inconvenient in practice and a general boundaries rule was substituted (Land Transfer Act 1875, s.83(5)). The boundaries of properties in a registered title are now general boundaries, unless shown as determined in which case there is an entry on the individual title registers giving details, possibly with particulars on the title plans. A general boundary does not determine the exact line (Land Registration Act 2002, s.60(1), (2)). That is to say, although it may be clear that some physical feature is followed – such as a wall or a ditch – the exact position of the line on the plan does not indicate who owns the feature, or whether the boundary actually runs down one of the sides or down the middle of it.* As the Land Registry maps and plans often consist of or are based on Ordnance Survey maps, the boundary lines will normally be drawn down the middle of the physical features in accordance with Ordnance Survey practice. A broken line is often used on the Registry plans to indicate a boundary where no physical feature yet exists, as where a fence is still to be erected. Nevertheless, Land Registry plans are as precise as possible and no

---

* This sentence was cited in *Cutland v Atwell* (1994) unreported, *per* Peter Gibson L.J.

great variation from the boundary shown comes within the rule. *Lee v Barrey* [1957] Ch. 251, where the Court of Appeal held that a divergence of 10 feet was within the general boundaries rule, is considered exceptional. That particular filed plan bore an endorsement that it was subject to revision after the erection of fences, implying that it gave no more than a general indication of the boundaries.

Without being technically fixed boundaries, certain boundary features may be recorded on the register as either included in or excluded from the title. These precise indications are effective, but leave the general rule unaffected as far as the rest of the boundaries are concerned.

The filed plan may show "T" marks in two circumstances. First, when they are referred to in restrictive covenants, or in positive covenants imposed with restrictive ones and reproduced on the register with them. Secondly, in cases where they appeared on a plan referred to in a pre-registration deed, but without any explanation in the deed of their significance, and the applicant for first registration specifically requests their inclusion. In the latter case, the fact that the marks were not referred to in the deed will be recorded on the register. Before 1962 such "T" marks were not reproduced on filed plans.

(b) Determined boundaries

1–41 Only where there is an entry on the individual title register, possibly also with particulars on the title plan, giving details of a boundary of which the exact line is fixed, will the boundary be precise and fixed. Part only of a boundary may be fixed in this way (Land Registration Rules 2003, rr.117, 119). The obvious advantages are that those boundaries can be relied upon, and are guaranteed so that even the slightest adjustment by rectification could be the basis of an indemnity claim under the Land Registration Act 2002, Sch.8.

An application to determine the exact line of a boundary is made on Form DB (Land Registration Rules 2003, r.119). The procedure supersedes the former procedure for defining a fixed boundary. The application form must be accompanied by evidence, including evidence of any unregistered title to the adjoining land, and two copies of a plan or verbal description, which identifies the exact line of the boundary claimed, showing sufficient surrounding physical features to allow the general position to be drawn on the Ordnance Survey. There is no Land Registry fee for an application to determine a boundary that accompanies an application to register a transaction, which attracts a scale fee. In other cases there is a fixed fee.

The Registry advises that the scale of the plan be no smaller than 1/200. The plan should be no larger than A3; more than one may be used if necessary. Measurements on it must be precise and accurate to 10 mm, and they must be made from a precise point on a physical feature such as the corner of a building. Information and detail not required for recording the boundary should be omitted. A plan bearing any disclaimer statement is not acceptable. Generally, the Land Registry will have to make a detailed survey. But it may be possible to avoid this if the plan is endorsed with a certificate by the Ordnance Survey, a chartered land surveyor or another suitably qualified professional. The suggested certificate is, "I certify that the measurements on this plan are accurate to 10 mm".

The Registrar gives notice to adjoining owners who are affected. The application form makes provision for the adjoining owner to join in to agree the application. This concurrence is not essential, but is clearly very helpful.

The exact line of a boundary may be determined on the initiative of the Registrar without the landowner making an application (Land Registration Rules 2003, r.122). This may be done where there is a transfer or the grant of a lease of part of land in a registered title, a common boundary – between the land disposed of and the land of the person making the disposition – and sufficient information to determine the exact line of that common boundary.

(c) Registered boundary agreement
If adjoining landowners formally agree the position of a common   **1–42**
boundary, the Land Registry will make a note of the agreement on the titles concerned. However, this is not a determination of the exact line of the boundary and will not necessarily be binding on other parties.

An agreement may relate to the treatment of accretion or diluvion. It can be noted on the property register after an application has been made with the consent of the proprietors of the registered estate and any registered charge who are not parties to the agreement (Land Registration Rules 2003, s.123).

7 Commons

The registration of common land and town and village greens under   **1–43**
the Commons Registration Act 1965 involved a determination of their boundaries, and consequently the boundaries of the adjoining private properties. Registrations are by reference to plans, and the documents are open to public inspection. The register is conclusive evidence of the matters registered, as at the date of registration (s.10). This includes the extent of the land. The boundary of land to be registered as waste land of a manor does not alter, when bounded

by the sea, when gradual imperceptible accretions change the shore line (*Baxendale v Instow Parish Council* [1982] Ch. 14).

The Countryside Agency and the Countryside Agency for Wales have a duty to prepare maps showing, respectively in England (outside Inner London) and in Wales, first all registered common land and secondly all open country (land that consists wholly or predominantly of mountain, moor, heath or down and is not common land). After time for an appeal procedure, the agencies can be directed to publish maps in conclusive form. A certified copy of a conclusive map may be received in evidence (Countryside and Rights of Way Act 2000, ss.1, 4, 9). No conclusive map has yet been published. The progress of mapping in England may be checked on the Countryside Agency's website, *www.countryside.gov.uk*.

8 Variation of boundaries

(a) By agreement

1–44   Adjoining landowners may fix or alter their boundaries by agreement. A variation of boundaries amounts to an assurance of the land involved. A deed is therefore necessary (LPA 1925, s.52), and if the title is registered the prescribed form of Land Registry transfer must be used. An agreement to complete a deed of variation or a transfer for this purpose must be in writing and comply with the requirements of the Law of Property (Miscellaneous Provisions) Act 1989, s.2. The only restrictions on the power of a landowner to agree to alter his boundaries are those general restrictions on any disposition of land imposed on certain bodies, or persons under a disability.

If, however, the boundary was previously in doubt, and the agreement is a genuine attempt to state what is thought always to have been the position, neither a deed, nor even writing, is necessary because no land changes hands. Indeed, an agreement need not be express, but may be inferred from the circumstances. Examples are: the surveyor acting for a seller approved the siting of a new boundary fence that the buyer covenanted to erect (*Stephenson v Johnson* [2000] E.G.C.S. 92); neighbours who were obliged to separate their properties by a wall acquiesced in the erection of a new wall in a slightly different place (*Burns v Morton* [2000] 1 W.L.R. 347).

For the same reason the agreement is not registrable as an estate contract under the Land Charges Act 1972, unless it intends to vary a boundary (*Neilson v Poole* (1969) 20 P. & C.R. 909). The settlement is sufficient mutual consideration to make the agreement enforceable (*Penn v Lord Baltimore* (1750) 1 Ves. Sen. 444). Clearly, however, a deed accurately recording the settled boundaries for the future is more satisfactory.

(b) Adverse possession
If one landowner encroaches on some of the land of his neighbour 1–45
in circumstances that amount to adverse possession, he can acquire ownership of the land on which he squatted. This necessarily varies the boundaries between the two properties (*Williams Bros Direct Supply Ltd v Raftery* [1958] Q.B. 159). This applies even if the owner's right to recover possession is subject to statutory restriction (*e.g.* under the Rent Act) (*Moses v Lovegrove* [1952] 2 Q.B. 533). Acquisition by prescription can vary the presumptions to which reference may be made when determining boundaries (*e.g.* where there is a hedge and a ditch) (*Marshall v Taylor* [1895] 1 Ch. 641). But if the acts of purported ownership are not sufficient to establish adverse possession, a fence can lawfully be re-erected along the original boundary (*Dear v Woods* (1984) 9 C.S.W. 728).

The requirements and procedure vary, however, depending on whether the title to the land in question has a registered title. In both cases, the requirement of adverse possession is the same. The occupier must enjoy the land in a way that is inconsistent with the other's ownership. Archetypically, this involves fencing in the occupied land, but that will not necessarily suffice (*e.g. Wilson v Martin's Executors* [1993] 1 E.G.L.R. 178). The squatter must assert his ownership and what satisfies that requirement depends on the facts.

In the case of registered land – and subject to transitional provisions where a squatter acquired a title before October 13, 2003 – the squatter must apply to be registered as proprietor of the land in question after he has occupied it for at least 10 years (Land Registration Act 2002, Sch.6, para.1). Ownership does not change hands until the register is amended. On the other hand, adverse possession of unregistered land for 12 years automatically vests the title in the squatter without more (Limitation Act 1980, s.15(1)). In both cases, the period of adverse possession that is required is extended where the land is Crown property or foreshore.

(c) Estoppel
A landowner's act, or that of a predecessor in title, may stop him 1–46
from taking action in respect of an encroachment upon his boundaries that has the practical effect of varying the boundaries, at any rate as between those parties and persons deriving title under them. So where a company that owned one of two adjacent plots agreed with the owner of the other to build a house and garage on it in such a position that the garage encroached upon the company's plot by between two and three feet, the company's successor in title could

not maintain an action for trespass against a subsequent owner of the garage (*Hopgood v Brown* [1955] 1 W.L.R. 213).

(d) Rectification

1-47 Where the parties to a binding agreement purport to carry it into effect by a document which is not in accordance with the agreement, that document can be rectified. This principle can apply to vary boundaries of land defined by a conveyance, if they do not accord with what the parties agreed in their prior contract (*Craddock Brothers Ltd v Hunt* [1923] 2 Ch. 136).

In certain circumstances the land register may be rectified, which includes a title plan (Land Registration Act 2002, Sch.4). This may be the result of a court order or the alteration may be made by the Registrar. The purpose may be to correct a mistake, to update the register or to give effect to an estate, right or interest excepted from the effect of registration. The Registrar may also remove a surplus entry.

(e) Inclosure Acts

1-48 The inclosure of commons, which necessarily involves the definition of new boundaries, is not a subject that can be dealt with here. It must be mentioned, nevertheless, that a valuer appointed under the Inclosure Act 1845 has power, with the consent of adjoining owners, to straighten fences or define new boundaries of the lands to be inclosed or regulated, and to give directions for the fencing of the new boundary (s.45). This procedure is, however, virtually obsolete because it is extremely elaborate, including calling local meetings and promoting a private Act of Parliament. Other provisions in the many statutes governing inclosure can affect boundaries. They are administered by the Department for Environment, Food and Rural Affairs, who may be able to give help.

(f) Natural forces

1-49 The gradual effects of wind and tide can alter the position of a boundary that is defined by reference to a physical feature such as a river bank or seashore. This does not apply where a single, unusually violent, natural phenomenon drastically and suddenly alters the position of river bed (*Ford v Lacey* (1861) 7 H. & N. 151), but merely to imperceptible accretions. Those accretions can, however, be large enough to provide an easily measurable difference over, say, a year (*R. v Lord Yarborough* (1824) 3 B. & C. 668).

The change in the position of the boundary applies equally to accretions and to erosion or dilution. Accretions to land bounded by the sea belong to the owner of that land (*Government of the State of Penang v Beng Hong Oon* [1972] A.C. 425), and erosion returns the land to Crown ownership (*Re Hull and Selby Railway* (1839) 5 M. & W. 139). The action of wind in blowing sand has been treated in the same way as alluvial accretions (*Southern Centre of Theosophy Inc. v State of South Australia* [1982] A.C. 706).

Even though land is registered with a particular boundary, this does not affect the operation of accretion or diluvion that may vary it (Land Registration Act 2002, s.61(1)).

Chapter 2

Sale of Land

1 Pre-contract

(a) Searches and enquiries
It is customary for prospective buyers to ascertain from the seller as   **2–01**
to the ownership of boundary features, and as to disputes which will
include boundary disputes. Failure to disclose a dispute in reply to a
preliminary enquiry can be a misrepresentation justifying the subsequent rescission of the contract (*Walker v Boyle* [1982] 1 W.L.R.
495). A buyer's solicitor who fails to pursue enquiries to find the
full facts about fences can be guilty of negligence (*McManus
Developments Ltd v Barbridge Properties Ltd* [1992] E.G.C.S. 50).
  Other pre-contract searches that can be important in relation to
boundary features are:

(1) Ownership of fences adjoining a railway line.

(2) Whether the local planning authority has made a direction
    under art.4 of the Town and Country Planning General
    Development Order 1988, restricting the general permission
    given for the erection of fences etc. One of the standard
    enquiries of local authorities to accompany local land charge
    searches refers to this, but it should be noted that it relates
    only to directions made by the council. In appropriate cir-
    cumstances, a direction can be made by a joint planning
    board, an urban development corporation or an enterprise
    zone authority.

(b) Misdescription
Conveyancing contracts normally seek to restrict the purchaser's   **2–02**
right to rescind on the ground of misrepresentation (*e.g. Standard
Conditions of Sale*, 4th edn, cond. 7.1, *Standard Commercial Property
Conditions*, 2nd edn, cond. 9.1). How far such a condition is effective

depends on the circumstances of each case. It must satisfy the test of reasonableness, *i.e.* the term must be a fair and reasonable one to be included having regard to the circumstances that were, or ought reasonably to have been, known to or in the contemplation of the parties when the contract was made (Misrepresentation Act 1967, s.3; Unfair Contract Terms Act 1977, ss.8(1), 11(1)).

In one case, auction particulars contained a colour photograph of the premises, wrongly showing the boundary to include too much property. The same conditions contained the term, "The property is believed and should be taken to be accurately described . . . and any error, omission or misstatement . . . shall not annul the sale . . .". That clause did not prevent the buyer rescinding because the seller could not be said to have believed that the property was correctly described, and the term was not fair and reasonable (*St Marylebone Property Co. Ltd v Payne* [1994] 2 E.G.L.R. 25 (CC)).

2 Title

(a) Proof of extent of property

2–03 A buyer has a right to a marketable title to the property sold by the contract, subject to any contrary terms in the contract. That involves establishing first the extent of what the seller contracts to sell, and secondly the boundaries of the land to which he deduces title. A contract normally defines the land sold in the particulars, and may refer to a plan. Even a plan that is not referred to in the contract may be used to determine what is sold, if it is handed to the purchaser with that intention (*Re Lindsay and Forder's Contract* (1895) 72 L.T. 832).

The courts are loath to deprive the buyer of his right to insist that the property to which title is offered is the same in extent as that which the seller contracted to sell. Contractual conditions that could prejudice that right are narrowly construed. In one case where the descriptions of the property in the various title deeds differed, and none was the same as the contract description, there was a condition of sale, "that no further evidence of the identity of the parcels shall be required, than what is afforded by the abstract, or the deeds, instruments, or other documents therein abstracted". Although the buyer could call for no further evidence, because of the effect of that condition, the vendor had not fulfilled his obligation to identify what he was selling and so could not oblige the purchaser to complete (*Flower v Hartopp* (1843) 6 Beav. 476). In another case, the contract provided that "the purchaser is not to require any further proof of identity than is furnished in the title deeds themselves", but the deeds did not identify the property. Again, the buyer could not require further evidence, but the seller could not oblige him to buy (*Curling v Austin* (1862) 2 Dr. & Sm. 129).

A contract condition, in the *National Conditions of Sale*, 17th edn, that the purchaser should admit the identity of the property with that comprised in the documents of title on the evidence of the descriptions in those deeds was considered in *Re Bramwell's Contract, Bramwell v Ballards Securities Investments Ltd* [1969] 1 W.L.R. 1659. The contract description of the property sold and the parcels in the root of title could only be reconciled as a matter of probability. As the deeds did not contain what could properly be called a description of the property for the purpose of the condition, it did not have any effect.

(b) Ownership of boundary features
Whether or not the seller owns the fences, etc., surrounding the property sold will only have a very small effect on the extent of the property sold, although disputes about ownership of and the responsibility to maintain boundary features can lead to considerable acrimony. The *Standard Conditions of Sale*, 4th edn, cond. 4.4.1, and the *Standard Commercial Property Conditions*, 2nd edn, cond. 6.4.1, provide:

2–04

The seller need not:

(a) prove the exact boundaries of the property;

(b) prove who owns fences, ditches, hedges or walls . . .

further than he may be able to do from the information in his possession.

The buyer has the right, when it is reasonable, to require the seller to make or obtain, pay for and hand over a statutory declaration as to the facts (cond. 4.4.2).

(c) Deducing title
A plan referred to in an abstracted deed relating to unregistered land is an integral part of the deed and the seller must supply a copy of it at his own expense (*Llewellyn v Earl of Jersey* (1843) 11 M. & W. 183). This is subject to the qualification that the plan must be necessary for properly identifying the property or correctly interpreting the deed. The Council of the Law Society decided that a purchase at auction of 20 acres of land, which the seller had purchased as part of an estate of 275 acres, was only entitled to a copy of that part of the original conveyance plan which related to the land he had bought (*Law Society's Digest*, vol.1, Opn 84, 1900).

2–05

The extent of registered land is briefly defined on the register, with a reference to the filed plan. Both the verbal description and the plan are therefore needed to determine the boundaries of the property (subject always to the general boundaries rule). The *Standard Conditions of Sale*, 4th edn, cond. 4.1.2, and the *Standard Commercial Property Conditions*, 2nd edn, cond. 6.1.2, require the seller to provide official copies, the individual register and any title plan.

(d) Not enough land

2–06 When the examination of title discloses that the seller is not in a position to sell all the land that he has contracted to, the buyer's remedies will depend on the terms of the contract. Under an open contract, or in the absence of express conditions of sale referring to the matter, the buyer is entitled to rescind if the extent of the property differs substantially from that contracted to be sold. Where the boundary is only slightly different, the purchaser's only remedy is compensation. This must be claimed before completion, otherwise he is taken to have waived his rights.

A deficiency in area of 40 per cent justifies rescission (*Watson v Burton* [1957] 1 W.L.R. 19). Where a property was described as including a wall and trademan's entrance, but actually excluded the wall and gave no indefeasible right to use the entrance, the right also arose (*Brewer v Brown* (1884) 28 Ch. D. 309). Even though the purchaser is entitled to rescind, he may nevertheless insist on taking a conveyance at a reduced price, the compensation being assessed at a fair figure, not a penal one.

The *Standard Conditions of Sale*, 4th edn, cond. 7.1, and the *Standard Commercial Property Conditions*, 2nd edn, cond. 9.1, contain provisions with the object of eliminating claims for compensation where discrepancies are immaterial, and restricting the buyer's rights to compensation rather than rescission in more substantial cases. Whether the right to rescind is successfully excluded in any particular case depends on whether the condition satisfies the test of reasonableness (Misrepresentation Act 1967, s.3; Unfair Contract Terms Act 1977, ss.8(1), 11(1)).

3 Conveyance

(a) Registered land

2–07 When dealing with the whole of the land in a registered title, the only description that is needed in the transfer, and the contract leading to it, is a reference to the title number. On a transfer of part, however, a plan is required (Land Registration Rules 2003, r.213(1)). The two prescribed forms, TP1 and TP2, offer the alternatives of defining the land transferred by attaching a plan or referring to the transferor's title plan if the area in question is delineated on it.

The rules require that a plan clearly identifies the land dealt with and the Registry has published requirements with which a plan should comply (*Practice Guide 40: Land Registry plans*, para.6.7). It should have sufficient detail to allow identification on the Ordnance Survey map and be drawn to scale: 1/1250–1/500 preferred for urban properties or 1/2500 preferred for urban properties, with a larger scale or inset plan for intricate boundaries. A plan should not be based on imperial measurements, and if measurements are shown, they should be in metric units to two decimal places. It should show: roads, road junctions and landmarks to give the general location; buildings, actual or intended, in their correct position and the land included; floor levels, where appropriate. The following are not acceptable: edgings of a thickness that obscures other detail; a reference that the plan is for identification only; a disclaimer statement under the Property Misdescriptions Act 1991.

(b) Unregistered land

The buyer is entitled to have the land conveyed to him by a modern description. This need not be the description by which was conveyed to the seller (*Re Sansom and Narbeth's Contract* [1910] 1 Ch. 741), nor need it be identical to the contract description. The buyer can insist on the inclusion of measurements, even when there was none in the contract description of the property, if this will avoid litigation which would be likely without them (*Monighetti v Wandsworth Borough Council* (1908) 73 J.P. 91).

2–08

On the other hand, the buyer can require that the contract description is repeated in the conveyance, if the alternative would be to exclude part of the land he contracted to buy (*Lloyd v Stanbury* [1971] 1 W.L.R. 535).

A buyer can generally insist on the conveyance referring to a plan if the verbal description is not adequate. When the words give a sufficient and satisfactory identification of the land sold, fixing all its boundaries, no plan is necessary (*Re Sharman's Contract* [1936] 1 Ch. 755). A whole island off the coast was satisfactorily described by naming it and referring to two other islands by name, and without referring to a plan showing an outline and measurements (*Collector of Land Revenue, Singapore v Hoalim* [1978] A.C. 525).

If the verbal description is not adequate, the buyer is entitled to a plan. That plan must be to an adequate scale (*Scarfe v Adams* [1981] 1 All E.R. 843). For a house, a scale of 1:1250 will generally suffice (*R. v Secretary of State for the Environment, ex parte Norwich City Council* [1982] Q.B. 808). The only exception is where a plan would be particularly complicated and might itself induce litigation. The duty to provide a plan applies even if the contract did not refer to one. Even though the contract plan was stated to be for reference only and without any guarantee of accuracy, the buyer can insist on its being used without those qualifications, if the plan is required to complete a satisfactory definition of the property conveyed (*Re Sparrow and James' Contract* [1910] 2 Ch. 60).

Chapter 3

Boundary Disputes

If there is any border land over which the precise boundary line is
obscure, it is usually something of very trifling value
*Report: Land Transfer Commission on the Operation of the Land
Registry Act (1870).*

There are few disputes that raise passions more than boundary
disputes
Clarke v O'Keefe (1997) 80 P. & C.R.126 *per* Peter Gibson L.J.

1 Types of action

(a) General

In default of agreement to submit them to arbitration, boundary dis-   **3–01**
putes can be brought before the courts for determination in a number of ways. If the position of the boundary is the only question in
issue a declaration may be sought. This jurisdiction is discretionary.
There must be nothing to disentitle the plaintiff to relief, and the
defendant must previously have asserted some right or formulated
some specific claim. The rule was that the court would not usually
entertain an action where the subject matter is under £10 in value
(*Westbury-on-Severn Rural Sanitary Authority v Meredith* (1885) 30
Ch. D. 387); that limit would surely now be higher. Where the question in issue is the interpretation of a deed, will or other document,
which may well be the case in a boundary dispute, any person interested may apply for a declaration of the rights of all the persons
interested. The application in boundary disputes, as matters of title,
will be to the Chancery Division.

An application for a declaration is usually linked with some other
form of action. The appropriate form where one party alleges
infringement of his boundary and occupation of part of his land
by the other is trespass. It is nuisance where the infringement

consists of allowing such things as tree roots to spread past his
boundary. The exact position of a boundary may be important in
other actions too, for example under the rule in *Ryland v Fletcher*
(1868) L.R. 3 H.L. 330, straying animals, contract and recovery of
road charges.

An action for damages may be appropriate, where the violation of
a boundary has deprived the plaintiff of the use of some of his land.
Particulars of special damage must be given (*Ilkiw v Samuels* [1963]
1 W.L.R. 991). A claim for damages can be small provided it is
genuine (*Hatt & Co. (Bath) Ltd v Pearce* [1978] 1 W.L.R. 885).

3–02   Boundary disputes may, by an agreement made either at the time
of the difference or before, be referred to arbitration, when the
Arbitration Acts will apply.

An owner objecting to an encroachment onto his property, as
where his neighbouring builds across the boundary without authority, has the common law right of self-redress against the trespasser.
The intrusion can be removed. However, that right should not be
exercised where the consequences are disproportionate, and it ceases
when court action has been determined (*Burton v Winters* [1993]
1 W.L.R. 1077).

The right to take action for trespass arising from the violation of
a boundary can be lost by inaction. The circumstances are viewed
broadly. They must make it unconscionable to allow the claimant to
deny what, knowingly or unknowingly, he has allowed or encour-
aged the defendant to assume, to his detriment (*Habib Bank Ltd v
Habib Bank AG Zurich* [1981] 1 W.L.R. 1265 at 1285). Simply allowing a neighbour to use a boundary wall for five years, although he
had no right to do so, may not be enough to establish this defence
(*Jones v Stones* [1999] 1 W.L.R. 1739).

(b) Registered land

3–03   Where the title to land of which the boundary is in dispute is registered, application may be made by one party to the Registrar for
rectification of the register. This would cover, for instance, misinter-
pretation of deeds when the title was investigated for first registration. Where, however, a strip of land is, by a mistake, conveyed twice
and the second purchaser registered as proprietor of it, justice may
prevent rectification to adjust the boundary once the registered
land has changed hands again (*Epps v Esso Petroleum Co. Ltd* [1973]
1 W.L.R. 1071).

A contested application to the Registrar for rectification that cannot be disposed of by agreement, may be referred to the Adjudicator
to H. M. Land Registry (Land Registration Act 2002, ss.73(7),
108(1)). There is an appeal to the High Court from a decision of the
Adjudicator (s.111(1)).

If this jurisdiction proceeds in the same way as hearings before the Registrar or the Solicitor to the Land Registry, under the Land Registration Act 1925, it may not be entirely satisfactory for settling disputes. For instance, a determination by the Registrar that construed a title deed to decide its effect on the entries on the register, did not preclude the court from construing the same deed in a different sense in subsequent proceedings between the same parties where more evidence is available (*Re Dances Way, West Town, Hayling Island* [1962] Ch. 490). Disputes affecting registered land may be brought before the courts in the usual way. Should the boundary be found to be different from that shown on the register, the court may order the Land Registry to effect the necessary rectification.

2 Evidence of the position of boundaries

The primary evidence available in boundary disputes is the title deeds to the properties. Extrinsic evidence is not available to vary a clear description given in a deed (*Scarfe v Adams* [1981] 1 All E.R. 843), but it may be called to lay before the court the information that the parties had at the time of the execution of the deed. It is also admissible in cases of ambiguity, even if only latent, *i.e.* only apparent when the deed is read by a person with knowledge of the facts. Evidence can be called to show the boundaries of the land as used prior to the grant, to prove what was meant to have been conveyed. Extrinsic evidence was admitted where land was transferred by reference to a plan, but because that plan was on an unsuitably small scale it was not unambiguous (*Clark v O'Keefe* (1997) 80 P. & C.R. 126). Similarly, where the plan attached to a deed was photocopied from an architect's plan, with the result that it was distorted and to no recognisable scale, the architect's plan was admitted as evidence (*Partridge v Lawrence* [2004] 1 P. & C.R. 14).

3–04

Evidence of reputation is only admissible where matters of general or public interest are concerned (*Evans v Merthyr Tydfil Urban Council* [1890] 1 Ch. 241; *Mercer v Denne* [1905] 2 Ch. 538). This would include boundaries of towns and parishes, and would only be of use in private boundary disputes where the extent of the land is defined by reference to such public boundaries. When admissible, such evidence may be oral or documentary. It may also consist of the verdict of a jury in a previous action between different parties (*Evans v Rees* (1839) 10 Ad. & El. 151).

3–05

(a) Civil Evidence Act 1995

3–06   A statement in a document which is admissible evidence (hearsay is no longer excluded: Civil Evidence Act 1995, s.1(1)) may be proved by producing the document or an authenticated copy of all or part of it (s.8).

(b) Business and public records

3–07   A document forming part of the records of a business or a public authority may be received in evidence without further proof (Civil Evidence Act 1995, s.9(1)).

(c) Public documents

3–08   The common law rules concerning the use of public documents as evidence have been preserved, notwithstanding the enactment of the new statute (Civil Evidence Act 1995, s.7(2)(*b*)).

The contents of public documents may generally be proved as evidence of the facts in them. Examples of such documents that have been received in evidence to prove boundaries include Domesday Book (being a record of a public survey) (*Alcock v Cooke* (1829) 5 Bing. 340; *Duke of Beaufort v John Aird & Co.* (1904) 20 T.L.R. 602); a survey made under a statutory duty, *e.g.* a tithe map and tithe apportionment survey (*Knight v David* [1971] 1 W.L.R. 1671); evidence of a tithe map was adduced in the Court of Appeal (*Minting v Ramage* [1991] E.G.C.S. 12); an ancient survey of Crown lands (*Doe d. William IV v Roberts* (1844) 13 M. & W. 520); and a map drawn by authority of a royal commission (*New Romney Corporation v New Romney Sewers Commissioners* [1892] 1 Q.B. 840). The survey must normally have been made with the intention that it should be available for public inspection, and the person undertaking it must be a public officer with a quasi-judicial duty to inquire into the matters recorded. It should be produced from proper custody.

A planning permission has been held to be a relevant public document (*Scott v Martin* [1987] 1 W.L.R. 841). A consent with a plan could be referred to as evidence of the background facts against which a conveyance should be construed (*Stock v David Wilson (Homes) Anglia Ltd* [1993] C.L.Y. 527).

Surveys not intended for public inspection, or made under private auspices, are not available as public documents. This includes Crown surveys made for private or temporary purposes such as a survey by the Augmentation Office for the Crown as a private owner (*Phillips v Hudson* (1867) 2 Ch. App. 243), and a seventeenth century survey of coastal castles to consider whether repairs were necessary (*Mercer v Denne* [1905] 2 Ch. 538). Such documents may, however, be admissible as a declarations of a deceased person.

(d) Ancient documents
Ancient documents produced from proper custody, which on the   **3–09**
face of them deal with questions of ownership, may be admitted in
evidence to prove boundaries. Examples are leases, or documents
showing that a person in occupation successfully protected his right
to possession. There is a presumption relating to such documents
produced from proper custody that are over 20 years old, in favour
of their validity: erasures and interlineations are presumed to have
been made before execution. This includes documents in the keeping
of a person to whom they came in the natural course.

(e) Title deeds
The title deeds of the properties divided by a disputed boundary will   **3–10**
be most important as evidence, and in an action a party is entitled to
discovery of deeds in the other party's possession, which either contain evidence of the joint title, or tend to substantiate the case of the
party seeking discovery. A party may resist discovery in boundary
cases only if the deeds relate exclusively to the case of the party
resisting or are immaterial (which is unlikely in this type of case).
Even then, a person who has been responsible for confusing the
boundaries cannot resist discovery. In disputes between landlord and
tenant, when the tenant has confused his own land with that demised
to him, the tenant must produce his own title deeds to the landlord.
The former rule that a third party called as a witness was entitled to
refuse to produce his title deeds, unless he or his predecessor in title
had given an acknowledgement for production to the party calling
him, or his predecessor in title, no longer applies (Civil Evidence Act
1968, s.16(1)(*b*)).

(f) Ecclesiastical terriers
An ecclesiastical terrier is a schedule of the temporal possessions of   **3–11**
a parish church. They are made from time to time. If produced from
proper custody, they are admissible in evidence, and may be of use
in proving the boundaries of glebe or adjoining lands. Proper custody would be the diocesan record office, the bishop's or the
archdeacon's registry or the chest of the parish church.

(g) Cathedrals
The precinct of each Church of England cathedral (other than   **3–12**
Christ Church, Oxford) is marked on a plan lodged with the Cathe-
drals Fabric Commission for England (Care of Cathedrals Measure
1990, s.13(4)). The address of the Commission is Church House,
Great Smith Street, London, SW1P 3BL (tel: 020 7898 1863).

(h) Ordnance Survey

3–13 Authority to carry out a complete survey of Britain and publish maps was first conferred by the Ordnance Survey Act 1841. The powers are now exercised by the Secretary of State for the Environment. Section 12 of the Act expressly provided that the powers conferred did not extend to ascertaining or altering private boundaries, and that private titles should remain unaffected. As such, the Ordnance Survey is not therefore of evidential value. It may, however, be adopted in private deeds and often is, in which case it is deemed to be incorporated in them and must be referred to. Many superseded Ordnance Survey maps are available as film or paper copies from Ordnance Survey, Romsey Road, Southampton, SO16 4GU (tel: 020 8030 5030), who will provide cost estimates for research and copying services. See also *www.ordnancesurvey.co.uk*. Some maps are kept in county record offices. Most are available in the British Library, and copies may be obtained, subject to paying a fee that will include any copyright payment.

(i) Other maps

3–14 Private boundaries may not be proved by maps attached to inclosure awards, which, although they may prove a road to be a highway, do not conclusively delineate its boundaries.

A map drawn, accepted or acted upon by a party to the proceedings or his predecessor in title, might be available as an admission of the facts shown, though not admissible as a public document. General maps and atlases may be adduced as evidence of facts within public knowledge.

It is unlikely that Land Registry plans would be used in evidence (except where the entries on them are directly in issue) because the boundaries shown are not normally precise. If it is desired to produce any plan filed in the Registry, an official copy is admissible to the same extent as the original (Land Registration Act 2002, s.67(1)).

(j) Declarations of deceased persons

3–15 In three cases relevant to boundary disputes the declarations of persons since deceased may be admitted in evidence: when against his pecuniary or proprietary interests; when made in the course of duty (*Price v Earl of Torrington* (1703) 1 Salk. 285); and when as to public rights. In the first case, the declaration must have been against the declarer's interests at that time, and have been so to his knowledge. To be admissible as made in the course of duty, the statement must concern his normal business, and be made in its normal course at or about the time to which it relates. This includes not only statements of a person holding permanent office, but also a professional (*e.g.* a surveyor) employed on an *ad hoc* basis for the particular job concerned (*Mellor v Walmesley* [1905] 2 Ch. 164). It is necessary for it to be apparent from the document that it was recorded as personal knowledge (not hearsay) and contemporaneously (*Mercer v Denne* [1905] 2 Ch. 538). Declarations as to public rights must have been made before any controversy arose. They must concern rights exercisable by the whole community (such as public rights of way) or a substantial part of it (such as a right of common), and such declarations must directly assert or deny the existence of the rights.

The effect of these provisions is to admit some documents that would otherwise be excluded. For example, surveys of Crown property made for the Crown's private purposes do not come within the definition of public documents for the purposes of admissibility, but if of some antiquity (so that the death of the author can be presumed without further proof, by reason of the normal life span) they will be available as evidence, by virtue of being a declaration made by a deceased person in the course of his duty.

(k) Acts of ownership

Evidence may be given of acts of ownership of property to establish boundaries. Acts which have been admitted include tree planting and felling, cutting grass, grazing cattle, fishing, turning off strangers or preventing them from removing soil. The perambulation of his boundaries by the lord of the manor is evidence of the extent of his manor.

3–16

If the dispute concerns the ownership of an existing boundary feature, or the question is whether the boundary is down one side or the other of it or down the middle, evidence of acts of ownership exercised over the feature is admissible. Such acts are clipping and trimming a hedge, repairing a fence or wall, or clearing a ditch.

Acts of ownership are not conclusive evidence, particularly if they are relatively slight and for the convenience of the person doing them. He might not have been under a legal obligation, or even have had the right, to do them. Acts carried out without the contesting neighbour's knowledge, and therefore without his acquiesence, are not good evidence (*Henniker v Howard* (1904) 90 L.T. 157).

(l) Mode of construction of boundary features

It is customary to build brick walls and close-boarded fences so that the piers and upright supports protrude onto the land of the owner of the wall or fence. This is so that the wall or fence may go right up to the boundary; if the protrusions were to project into the neighbour's property they would constitute a trespass that the owner could be made to remove. (Nevertheless, the foundations of party walls can project in certain cases.) Accordingly, that mode of construction of this type of wall or fence is *prima facie* evidence of its

3–17

ownership. But it is not conclusive, because owners are not compelled to build in this way: they may set the wall or fence back very slightly to avoid trespassing. A fence reversing the usual method of construction has the advantage that repairs can be carried out from the owner's side.

(m) Local custom

3–18 Occasionally local custom may help to establish the position of a boundary. For example, in one case it was alleged, but not established, that private properties that adjoined a common were always considered to extend four feet on the common side of their hedges so that a fence could be erected to protect the hedge from animals grazing on the common (*Collis v Amphlett* [1918] 1 Ch. 232; [1920] A.C. 271).

3 Introducing plans in evidence

3–19 In line with the general reforms of litigation practice, which encourage more openness and exchange of information between the parties, there are requirements that must normally be complied with by a party who wants to introduce a plan in evidence.

Advance warning must be given of the intention to use a plan as evidence at the hearing of an action, including a plan that is a business or public record and requires no further proof. The party intending to use it must give notice to the other parties before the hearing. Where the plan forms part of expert evidence, he must give notice when the expert's report is served. Otherwise, if it is not contained in a witness statement or affidavit and he intends to use it as evidence of a fact, notice must be served not later than the latest date for serving witness statements. Where there are not to be witness statements, or the plan is to be used solely to disprove an allegation in a witness statement, notice must be given at least 21 days before the hearing. Unless notice has been given, the plan can only be received in evidence if the court so orders (CPR Pt 33.6).

4 Seller and buyer

3–20 Under an open contract, or in the absence of express conditions of sale referring to this question, the buyer is entitled to rescind if the property differs substantially from that contracted to be sold. Where the boundary is only slightly different, the buyer's only right is compensation. This must be claimed before completion, otherwise the buyer is taken to have waived his rights. A deficiency in area of

40 per cent justifies rescission (*Watson v Burton* [1957] 1 W.L.R. 19), and where a property is described as including a wall and trademan's entrance, but excludes the wall and gives no indefeasible right to use the entrance, the right also arises (*Brewer v Brown* (1884) 28 Ch. D. 309). Even though the purchaser is entitled to rescind, he may nevertheless insist on taking a conveyance at a reduced purchase price, the compensation being assessed at a fair figure, not a penal one.

Contract terms may make provision with the object of restricting the parties' rights to compensation rather than rescission, except in cases of substantial discrepancies (*e.g. Standard Conditions of Sale*, 4th edn, cond. 7.1.3; *Standard Commercial Property Conditions*, 2nd edn, cond. 9.1.3). The extent to which the right to rescind is successfully restricted depends on whether the condition satisfies the reasonableness test (Misrepresentation Act 1967, s.3; Unfair Contract Terms Act 1977, ss.8(1), 11(1)).

5 Landlord and tenant

A tenant who impugns his landlord's title gives the landlord grounds for forfeiture of his lease, so boundary disputes, which are normally disputes as to title, are rare between landlord and tenant.   **3–21**

The relationship of landlord and tenant imposes an obligation upon the tenant to preserve the boundaries of the demised premises, and to prevent their being destroyed so that the landlord's property cannot be delimited (*Attorney-General v Fullerton* (1813) 2 Ves. & B. 263). Where the tenant has confused the boundaries by merging adjoining premises, the landlord may apply to the court to have the boundary ascertained, even during the term of the demise (*Spike v Harding* (1878) 7 Ch. D. 871). To give jurisdiction, the plaintiff must show by evidence, or the defendant's admission, that he has legal title to the land, that the boundaries are confused and that the tenant is in possession of part at least. If at the end of the term of a lease the boundaries are so confused that the tenant cannot render up precisely the landlord's property, he is bound to restore land of equal value. This is ascertained as fairly as may be, but doubts are resolved against the tenant, because he is at fault.

6 Crown lands

Formerly, special provisions applied to the settlement of disputes relating to Crown lands, and arbitration awards had to be enrolled in the Office of Land Revenue Records and Enrolments (now housed with and superseded by the National Archives (PRO), Kew, Richmond,   **3–22**

Surrey, KT9 4DU (tel: 020 8876 3444). These provisions were repealed by the Crown Estate Act 1961. In all Crown leases there is now inserted a provision for the Crown Estate Commissioners to settle boundary disputes. The address of the Commissioners is Crown Estate Office, 13–15 Carlton House Terrace, London, SW1Y 5AH (tel: 020 7210 4377).

7 Duchy of Cornwall lands

3–23   The Duke of Cornwall (or, during his minority, the Sovereign or other person appointed by her, on his behalf), with the previous consent of the Treasury, may make any arrangement to settle a boundary dispute affecting Duchy lands. The agreement must be enrolled in the Office of the Duchy of Cornwall, after which it is conclusive and binding on the Duke of Cornwall and all other interested parties. In the case of dispute as to the terms of such an agreement, the Duke of Cornwall may, with Treasury consent, agree to refer the matter to arbitration. The award must be enrolled in the Duchy Office, when it will be binding.

Enrolment is effected at the Duchy Office which is at 10 Buckingham Gate, London, SW1E 6LA (tel: 020 7834 7346), to which documents may be sent by post. Enrolment must be within six months of the date of the document, but enrolments out of time made *nunc pro tunc* may be permitted on reasonable cause being shown. A certificate of enrolment is admissible in all courts as proof of the original instrument and its enrolment.

Chapter 4

Party Walls

1 What is a party wall?

For the purposes of the Party Wall etc. Act 1996 a "party wall" is a **4–01**
wall separating buildings in different ownership or the wall of a
building standing partly on the land of one owner and partly on the
land of another. A "party fence wall" stands on lands in different
ownership but is not part of a building (s.20). These definitions are
dealt with below.

The 1996 Act aside, the term "party wall" is now applied to walls
dividing properties in different ownership in three situations: first,
where the wall is divided vertically in half, each neighbour owning
the half on his side; secondly, where the wall is entirely the property
of one adjoining owner, but is subject to easements or rights in
favour of the other to have it maintained dividing the properties;
thirdly, and most common, where the wall is divided vertically, but
each part is subject to cross-easements in favour of the other. These
different situations will be examined separately below. Before 1926
party walls were often held by the adjoining owners as tenants in
common, but in abolishing this form of joint ownership at law, the
LPA 1925 substituted a division of the wall with cross-easements.

(a) Vertically divided walls

A boundary wall that is built so that its centre exactly follows the **4–02**
dividing line will fall into this first class, being divided vertically into
halves each owned by the landowner adjoining it (*Matts v Hawkins*
(1813) 5 Taunt. 20). Even though it may be built at the joint expense
of the neighbours it is not subject to joint ownership. Whether the
wall is built exactly astride the boundary is a question of fact, but
minor inaccuracies will be ignored (*Reading v Barnard* (1827) Mood.
& M. 71).

The owner of one half of a wall that is divided in this way can,
in appropriate circumstances, acquire the other half by adverse

possession (*Prudential Assurance Co. Ltd v Waterloo Real Estate Inc.* [1999] 2 E.G.L.R. 85). In that case, the actions that successfully demonstrated the intention to possess the far side of the wall were: giving it the appearance of forming part of the claimant's premises, doing work on it that went beyond what could have been referable to an easement of support, raising the height of the wall and cleaning it, attaching security lighting and an entryphone system to it, cutting through the wall to insert a night safe and overflow pipe.

(b) Walls in single ownership

4–03 Where a boundary wall is built exclusively on the land of one owner it belongs to him in the absence of agreement to the contrary. The adjoining owner may acquire rights over it by agreement or prescription. (An easement of support may be acquired under the Prescription Act 1832 by user as of right for 20 years, provided that the owner of the servient tenement has not during the period been under a disability, or 40 years notwithstanding such disability.) Long use of a wall as part of a building on his land does not give the adjoining owner title to the wall (as it will not normally amount to exclusive possession of it adverse to the owner), but may give him an easement of support for his roof (*Waddington v Naylor* (1889) 60 L.T. 480). Acquisition of a wall by adverse possession can be avoided by fixing a notice to it visible to the public stating to whom it belongs.

(c) Divided walls subject to cross-easements

4–04 Walls expressly made subject to a tenancy in common, or since 1925 to the LPA 1925, s.38, or other walls not exclusively on one person's property (and not within the first class above), come within this class. In cases of doubt before 1926, there was a presumption that a tenancy in common existed. This applied, for instance, when the circumstances of building the wall and how much land each adjoining owner contributed were not known (*Cubitt v Porter* (1828) 8 B. & C. 257). Similarly, where both parties used the wall, this was sufficient *prima facie* evidence for the presumption to operate (*ibid.*).

Since 1925, cases where previously a tenancy in common existed or would have been created, and walls that are, or are expressed to be, party walls are covered by the LPA 1925, s.38. This provides that they shall be regarded as severed vertically, each part enjoying such rights of support and user over the other as would have subsisted if a valid tenancy in common of it had existed. These rights vary according to the circumstances, but normally extend to permitting the use of the wall by either adjoining owner for any purpose contemplated when the grant of the wall was made (*e.g.* support of a roof) without interference. A person interested in a party structure affected by the section may apply to the court for a declaration of the rights and interests of those interested, when the court may make such order as it thinks fit (LPA 1925, s.38(2)). Although the section refers to "walls or structures", its provision for dividing them vertically prevents it applying to ceilings and floors between flats and maisonettes in separate ownership.

2 Repairing party walls: overview

The repair obligations relating to a particular party wall may be governed by a contract between the parties in question or may arise under a lease. That aside, the right of one owner to repair a wall, which is not exclusively his, may arise under various provisions.

4-05

The Law of Property Act 1925, s.38, does not directly confer such rights. It in effect declares that cross-easements exist, and those easements confer rights at common law. The Access to Neighbouring Land Act 1922 offers a property owner who needs access to neighbouring property to do repairs the chance to obtain a county court order to authorise it. This applies to party wall repairs (*Dean v Walker* (1996) 73 P. & C.R. 366). Finally, the Party Wall etc. Act 1996 gives a property owner the right to repair a party wall.

The provisions applying to repairs in each of these three cases differ, and so do their consequences. It is also necessary to distinguish the separate authority to carry out new work that only the 1996 Act gives.

The position is summarised by Figure 4.1.

3 Party Wall etc. Act 1996

(a) Origin

The 1996 Act effectively extends to the whole country rules that have for many years applied in central London (London Buildings Act (Amendment) Act 1939). This local legislation was repealed when the general Act came into force (1996 Act, s.21(1)). Although there are some amendments to the London Act, many of the provisions remain the same. Accordingly, court decisions interpreting that Act should equally apply to the new one.

4-06

(b) Scheme of the Act

The aim of the 1996 Act is to maximise the use of property, while protecting adjoining owners. To this end, it gives property owners three sets of rights relating to walls on their boundaries and sometimes to floors that constitute the boundaries of their property. First, they have rights of repair; secondly, they may extend the use they

4-07

FIGURE 4.1

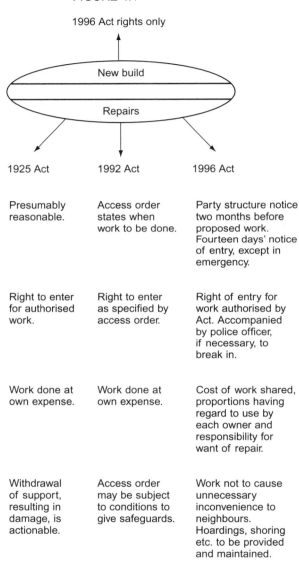

	1925 Act	1992 Act	1996 Act
Notice to be given	Presumably reasonable.	Access order states when work to be done.	Party structure notice two months before proposed work. Fourteen days' notice of entry, except in emergency.
Right of entry	Right to enter for authorised work.	Right to enter as specified by access order.	Right of entry for work authorised by Act. Accompanied by police officer, if necessary, to break in.
Cost of work	Work done at own expense.	Work done at own expense.	Cost of work shared, proportions having regard to use by each owner and responsibility for want of repair.
Safeguards	Withdrawal of support, resulting in damage, is actionable.	Access order may be subject to conditions to give safeguards.	Work not to cause unnecessary inconvenience to neighbours. Hoardings, shoring etc. to be provided and maintained.
Settlement of disputes	Application to court.	Access order only granted after county court application.	Statutory arbitration, appeal to county court.

make of the wall and do consequential construction work; thirdly, they can erect new walls on or over their boundaries. There are also restrictive provisions: an owner who wants to excavate on his own land may have to give prior notice to his neighbour in circumstances where the excavation might prejudice a structure on the neighbouring land.

Before exercising a statutory right an owner has to serve notice on the adjoining owner specifying what is proposed, and the adjoining owner has the right to challenge it by serving a counter-notice. This gives him the chance to suggest modifications to the proposed works, so that they are more useful to him. There are provisions for dispute resolution, and a subsequent appeal to the courts, if they disagree.

(c) Scope of the Act

The 1996 Act defines a number of the terms it uses. The definitions **4–08** are important, because they explain the circumstances which the Act covers.

The term "party wall" covers two cases. First, it is a wall, forming part of a building, which stands on lands in different ownership. This ignores a case where the overlap is merely the extent of artificial supports on which the wall rests. Secondly, it is that part of a wall that separates buildings in different ownership. This contrasts with a "party fence wall", which is a boundary wall that does not form part of a building. It must be used to separate the adjoining properties, or have been constructed for that purpose. It straddles the boundary, which means standing on lands in different ownership, to a greater extent than merely the artificial supports for the wall. A "party structure" extends the term "party wall" to include floor partitions and other structures separating buildings or parts of buildings approached by separate staircases or separate entrances (1996 Act, s.20). The equivalent definition in the London Act required the separate entrances to be "from without". Dropping those words make it clear that the Act is not only referring to parts of buildings with an entrance to the open air.

The 1996 Act uses "owner" in a broad sense, but the term does not include statutory tenants under the Rent Act 1977 (*Frances Holland School v Wassef* [2001] 2 E.G.L.R. 88 (CC), interpreting the London Building Act 1930, s.5, the scope of which was the same). Three categories fall within the definition. It includes (1996 Act, s.20):

(*a*) a person in receipt of the whole or part of the rents and profits of the property. This includes a long leaseholder, even though he has sublet for a term longer than from year to year (*Hunt v Harris* (1865) 19 C.B.(N.S.) 13);

(*b*) a person in possession of the land, but not as a mortgagee or as a tenant from year to year or a lesser term or a tenant at will;

(*c*) a contracting buyer or tenant, except under an agreement for a tenancy from year to year or for a lesser term.

This means that there may be more than one "owner" of a particular piece of land. Say, *e.g.* that *A* owns the freehold, previously let it to *B* for 99 years, who in turn sublet to *C* for 25 years, and *A* now contracts to sell the freehold to *D* subject to the leases: all four qualify as "owner".

4–09   A "building owner" is a landowner who wants to exercise statutory rights. He may own open land, rather than a building. All (or both) the owners of jointly owned property constitute the building owner: so, to be valid, a statutory notice must be given by all of them (*Lehmann v Herman* [1993] 1 E.G.L.R. 172). The same must apply to the "adjoining owner", but the difficulty of not knowing who owns premises can be overcome when serving a notice by addressing it to "the owner" of named premises (1996 Act, s.15(2)(*a*)).

The 1996 Act does apply to Crown land (s.19).

The only property to which the 1996 Act does not apply is land belonging to one of the Inns of Court in inner London (s.18) *i.e.* the boroughs of Camden, Greenwich, Hackney, Hammersmith, Islington, Kensington and Chelsea, Lambeth, Lewisham, Southwark, Tower Hamlets, Wandsworth and Westminster (London Government Act 1963, s.43).

(d) What an owner may do: existing structures

4–10   Where the boundary of adjoining properties in different ownership is built over, or there is a party fence wall or the external wall of a building on the boundary, the 1996 Act gives the owners extensive rights to do work on the existing structures (1996 Act, s.2). To exercise the rights he must follow the statutory procedure or have the adjoining owner's or occupier's written consent to his serving notices on the adjoining owner.

The work the owner may do is as follows (s.2). The authority is generally subject to an obligation to make good all damage to premises, internal furnishings and decorations, and in appropriate cases to raising flues and chimney stacks.

4–11   (*a*) Underpinning, thickening or raising a party structure or party fence wall, or his own external wall built against one of them.

If the work is necessary because of a defect or want of repair, the duty to make good does not apply. The cost is then shared in proportions reflecting responsibility for the defect or lack of repair and the use each owner makes of the wall or structure (s.11(4)).

(*b*) Making good, repairing, or demolishing and rebuilding a party structure or party fence wall that is defective or in need of repair.

(*c*) Exposing a party wall or party structure previously enclosed. Adequate weathering must be provided.

(*d*) Raising, lowering or rebuilding a party fence wall, including doing so to use it as a party wall. If the adjoining owner only uses it as a boundary wall, he can be called upon to contribute to the cost of requiring it to be more than two metres high (s.11(7)).

(*e*) Where a partition separates buildings in different ownership but does not comply with statutory requirements, demolishing the partition and replacing it with a party wall that does comply. Buildings connected by arches or other structures over a public way or someone else's passage may similarly be demolished and replaced if they do not comply with statutory requirements. A building and structure erected before July 18, 1996 (the day the Act was passed) is deemed to comply with statutory requirements if it complied when it was erected.

(*f*) Demolishing a party structure that is not strong or high enough for a proposed new building, and replacing it with one that is. The replacement need not be so high or thick, provided it serves the adjoining owner's purpose.

(*g*) Cutting into a party structure for any purpose (including inserting a damp proof course) or into the adjoining owner's wall to insert flashing or other weather proofing of another wall built against it.

(*h*) Cutting away projections to allow the building or underpinning of a party, party fence, external or boundary wall, or to enable the building owner to build a vertical wall against the adjoining owner's wall or building.

(e) Procedure

A building owner wishing to exercise any of these rights must serve a "party structure notice" on the adjoining owner at least two months before work is to begin. This specifies the nature and details

4–12

of the work proposed. Where there are to be foundations reinforced with steel rods or beams ("special foundations"), plans must also be served. The notice ceases to have effect if the work is not started within 12 months after it is served and prosecuted with diligence (1996 Act, s.3).

The adjoining owner has one month within which to serve a counter-notice. In the case of special foundations, the counter-notice may require them to be stronger and/or deeper to accommodate a new building for the adjoining owner. In other cases it may require the building of chimneys, flues, copings, piers or recesses for the adjoining owner's convenience. Plans of the works specified must accompany the notice.

The building owner must comply with the requirements of the counter-notice, unless they would be injurious to him, cause him unnecessary inconvenience, or unnecessarily delay the work (s.4).

(f) What an owner may do: new structures

4–13   The owner of land on one side of a boundary that is not built on, or where there is merely a boundary wall that is neither a party fence wall nor the external wall of a building, may build up to or straddling the boundary on following the statutory procedure (1996 Act, s.1).

An owner who wants to build a party wall or a party fence wall, extending across the boundary, must give at least one month's notice with details of his proposal. Only if the adjoining owner agrees (by serving notice within 14 days), can the wall be a party wall or a party fence wall. It is built half on the land of each owner, or in a different position that they agree, and the expense is shared in proportions having regard to each owner's use of the wall and the cost of labour and materials when they use it. If the adjoining owner does not agree to the wall being built across the boundary, the building owner must erect it wholly on his own land, at his own expense.

Even if a building owner proposes to build a wall on the boundary, but wholly on his own land, he must serve notice at least one month before work starts, describing the intended wall.

An owner building a boundary wall wholly on his own land – whether from choice or because the adjoining owner did not agree to a party wall or a party fence wall – may put projecting footings and foundations into the adjoining land during the year after he gave his notice. He must also compensate any adjoining owner or occupier for damage caused by building the wall and from making footings and foundations.

The requirements of the Act are mandatory. An interlocutory order, to remove new building work over the boundary line, was made against defendants who were aware of the equivalent procedure under the former London Building Acts, but did not follow it (*London & Manchester Assurance Co. Ltd v O & H Construction Ltd* [1989] 2 E.G.L.R. 185).

(g) Relationship to other obligations
A land owner may have other obligations which appear to run con-   **4–14**
trary to some of the rights given by the 1996 Act. For example, a restrictive covenant or a tenant's covenant in a lease may forbid any alteration to a boundary wall. The wording used by the Act in relation to existing structures, "A building owner shall have the following rights" (s.2(2)) suggests that, assuming the statutory procedure is followed, it overrides a private prohibition.

However, the Act operates to regulate the relations between the neighbouring owners or occupiers. Accordingly, although it may well govern relations between them, it would presumably not override bargains between a landowner and someone other than the neighbouring landowner. A landlord might or might not own or occupy adjoining land, and therefore the effect of the Act on a lease will vary. Further, the Act would presumably have no effect on other forms of regulation, *e.g.* conditions attached to a planning permission.

(h) Excavation
The Act is not confined to building work at the boundary between   **4–15**
properties in separate ownership. A building owner who excavates within three metres, and sometimes six metres, of a structure on adjoining land to below the level of that structure's foundations, may be called upon to underpin the structure or strengthen the foundations (1996 Act, s.6).

(i) Execution and cost of works
A building owner must not exercise his statutory rights in a way, or   **4–16**
at a time, which unnecessarily inconveniences any adjoining owner or occupier. If any part of the adjoining land or building is laid open, the building owner must maintain and pay for a proper hoarding or shoring as necessary to protect the property and for the security of the occupier (1996 Act, s.7). An adjoining owner may require the building owner to give security before starting work (s.12).

The building owner has a right to enter land and premises to do the work, as do his servants, agents and workmen, and to obstruct them is an offence (s.16). They must give 14 days' notice except in an emergency. They may stay during normal working hours, and may remove furniture and fittings and take other necessary action. In order to enter, they may break open fences and doors, if accompanied by a police officer (s.8).

The cost of authorised work is borne by the building owner, except where the Act provides for its being shared (s.11(1)).

(j) Disputes

4–17   There is a statutory procedure for settling all disputes between adjoining owners (1996 Act, s.10). Either they agree to appoint one surveyor ("agreed surveyor"), or each appoints his own and the two surveyors appoint a third, the three acting together. Appointments are made in writing and are irrevocable. There are provisions to cover cases where a party fails to appoint a surveyor or the surveyor fails to act or becomes incapable or dies. A surveyor appointed under this procedure has a right of entry to the premises during normal working hours (s.8(5)), and it is an offence to obstruct him (s.16).

For this purpose "surveyor" is anyone, other than a party, appointed to determine a dispute (s.20). The definition is therefore circular, but it certainly does not require any professional qualification.

The award to settle the dispute may determine what work may be done, how and when. It may also settle incidental matters and order the payment of reasonable costs. The award cannot settle future disputes between the parties, but it can impose continuing maintenance obligations (*Marchant v Capital & Counties plc* [1983] 2 E.G.L.R. 155). Nevertheless, the jurisdiction is limited to disputes concerning work authorised by the Act. It does not extend to related matters, *e.g.* damage caused by the collapse of a boundary wall during the period allowed for the adjoining owner to give consent to works (*Woodhouse v Consolidated Property Corporation Ltd* (1992) 66 P. & C.R. 234).

4–18   The agreed surveyor may make the award. Where there are three surveyors, two or three of them may make the award, or either of the parties, or their surveyors may call upon the third surveyor to do so.

An award is conclusive, but within 14 days of its delivery either party may appeal to the county court. The court's powers extend to rescinding or modifying an award. For that purpose, it can receive evidence of fact or opinion, including evidence not available to the surveyor(s) (*Chartered Society of Physiotherapy v Simmonds Church Smiles* [1995] 1 E.G.L.R. 155).

A party wall award does not appear to give the owner who benefits an interest in land. An award under the former London Building Acts (Amendment) Act 1939 authorised a building owner to excavate on the basis that he made good any damage to the neighbour's building, and in default the neighbour was given the right to enter to do the work at the landowner's expense. The neighbour's building was damaged, but he was not entitled to register a caution against dealings (under the Land Registration Act 1925) at H.M. Land

Registry (*Observatory Hill Ltd v Camtel Investments SA* [1997] 1 E.G.L.R. 140).

(k) Successor in title

The Act leaves a series of questions, as to the effect of one of the neighbouring properties changing hands, unanswered. The rights that a building owner can establish under the Act, either to erect a new building on a boundary (s.1) or in relation to an existing party structure (s.2), are described as rights to carry out certain works. The wording is appropriate for them to be rights *in rem*, exercisable whoever owns the adjoining land (unless, presumably, it becomes land to which the Act does not apply: s.18). Accordingly, there should be no difficulty once the statutory procedure has been completed. The right is exercisable on the adjoining land, whoever owns it. Presumably also it is exercisable by the owner for the time being of the "dominant" land, who by owning the land and desiring to do the work becomes the "building owner".   **4–19**

However, there is no express provision to bring the existence of a party wall agreement or award to the attention of later property owners. They are not registrable at the Land Registry, and as they do not relate to an owner's power of disposition there must be doubt whether a notice can properly be registered.

There may be greater difficulty if the adjoining land is transferred while the statutory procedure is still in progress. Is an incoming owner bound by notices served on or by his predecessor, or must the procedure start again? Again, there is no provision for registration to warn a buyer that something is afoot, although it is pre-contract information which the seller should divulge.

Other difficulties can arise if the building owner parts with his interest after giving security for the performance of statutory work (s.12). If his successor in title does not fully comply with his obligations can the adjoining owner have recourse to that security? Is the outgoing building owner bound to leave the security deposited? What are the rights of the former and later building owners against each other?

(l) Landlord and tenant

The rights of tenants may raise other queries. The Act's definition of "owner" clearly includes a tenant for a longer term than year to year (s.20). Accordingly, a tenant for a term of years who uses the statutory procedure obtains a right to carry out the work, which is enforceable against the adjoining owner. If that adjoining owner happens to be his landlord, there is little doubt that any contrary term in the lease is overridden. But if that is not the case, there seems no reason to suppose, as there is nothing to that effect in the statute,   **4–20**

that in dealing with the position between the tenant and his neighbour the Act negatives the effect of a lease covenant forbidding the
tenant to do the work he proposes.

The position is presumably the same if the landlord who owns
neighbouring property proposes to do work that he expressly
covenants in the lease not to do, or which might derogate from the
grant. He obtains statutory authority. However, it must be borne in
mind that a landlord's covenant for quiet enjoyment protects the
tenant against the lawful acts of others. That raises the question
whether a landlord exercising statutory rights could nevertheless be
liable for damages for breach of that covenant.

The Act defines "adjoining owner" to mean "any owner and any
occupier" of adjoining land (s.20). Presumably, this means that the
response to a building owner's statutory notice must come from all
those with interests in the adjoining land. This would include both
landlord and tenants, and here the use of the word "occupier" brings
in tenants with shorter terms. To ensure that they speak with the
same voice, landlords may consider including in leases a covenant
requiring the tenant to subscribe to any response they make. This
would mirror the common lease provision that requires the tenant to join in the landlord's response to applications for planning
permission relating to the development of neighbouring land.

4 Common law obligations

(a) Support

4–21   An easement of support for one part of a party wall by another in
separate ownership may be acquired by grant, express or implied, or
by prescription. In the absence of acquisition by any of these methods, there is no right of support (*Peyton v London Corporation* (1829)
9 B. & C. 725). If support is withdrawn by the adjoining owner, no
action lies for the resulting damage. This remains so even if the
building owner has covenanted with the neighbour who withdraws
the support to keep his building in repair, and the withdrawal makes
it impossible to comply with his covenant (*Colebeck v The Girdlers
Company* (1876) 1 Q.B.D. 234).

Cases now falling under s.38 of the LPA 1925 will have such an
easement, and where part of a wall is granted by the owner to his
neighbour with the intention of making it a party wall, the grant and
reservation is implied of such cross-easements as are necessary to
carry out the parties' intentions for the joint use of the wall (which
will vary according to the facts of each case) (*Jones v Pritchard*
[1908] 1 Ch. 630, 635). This right binds a local authority that demolishes the servient tenement under a clearance order, even though it

acts under a statutory duty, and accordingly it must provide alternative support (*Bond v Nottingham Corporation* [1940] Ch. 429). Where
the ownership of the wall is split vertically without mutual rights,
neither half is entitled to support from the other. Rights of support
exist only where houses adjoin, so the demolition of the next but one
house in a terrace is not an actionable withdrawal of support
(*Solomon v Vintners' Co.* (1859) 5 H. & N. 585). Nevertheless, in cases
where no easement of support exists, an action in negligence may be
maintained where damage is caused by the adjoining owner's failure
to observe a proper standard of care (*St Anne's Well Brewery Co. v
Roberts* (1928) 140 L.T. 1).

Where support is wrongfully withdrawn, the action will be for nui-   **4–22**
sance. Even where damage has been suffered, the adjoining owner is
not liable for merely failing to keep his building or part of the wall
in repair, only for positive acts resulting in the withdrawal of support
(*Sack v Jones* [1925] Ch. 235). In these cases he is equally liable for
the acts of independent contractors engaged by him (*Bower v Peate*
(1876) 1 Q.B.D. 321). The adjoining owner who is liable continues to
be so even though he may sell his property before some or all of the
resulting damage becomes apparent. The occupier who succeeds him
is not liable (*Hall v Duke of Norfolk* [1900] 2 Ch. 493).

In the case of a boundary wall in single ownership, there will be
an easement for natural support, but this relates only to the support
of the soil. A withdrawal of support for the wall is in such a case,
therefore, only actionable if it is such as to cause a greater than min-
imal fall of soil, whatever the effect on the wall. In addition, there
may be an easement for the support of the wall itself, acquired by
grant or prescription. Such an easement is extinguished if the dominant owner alters the use of the wall in a way substantially to prejudice the enjoyment of the servient tenement (*Ray v Fairway Motors
(Barnstaple) Ltd* (1969) 20 P. & C.R. 261).

(b) Repairs
An easement of support does not cast upon the joint owner of a   **4–23**
party wall any positive obligation to keep his part of the wall in
repair. Similar duties may nevertheless arise as a result of the law of
nuisance. If a party wall collapses because of neglect by one owner,
the other has no right of action (*Sack v Jones* [1925] Ch. 235). The
other owner need not, however, sit by and watch the wall crumble,
but may enter his neighbour's property in order to carry out repairs
(*Bond v Nottingham Corporation* [1940] Ch. 429, 439). Where the
easement is one of support only, without any additional repairing
obligation, there is no right to reimbursement for the cost of repairs
to someone else's wall (*The Highway Board, etc., of Macclesfield v
Grant* (1882) 51 L.J.Q.B. 357).

One property owner protected his building from exposure to the
weather through a party wall, following the demolition of the neighbouring building, by building eaves out over the neighbour's land.
He successfully resisted an application for a mandatory injunction to
remove the eaves, because the court exercised its discretion taking
into account the neighbour's conduct (*Tollemache & Cobbold Brew-
eries v Reynolds* [1983] 2 E.G.L.R. 158).

An adjoining owner is entitled to make use of a party wall for the
purpose originally intended. If in doing so the neighbouring property is damaged, he is not liable (*Jones v Pritchard* [1908] 1 Ch. 630).
If one of the owners demolishes and rebuilds for such purposes, he
is bound to see that the operations are carried out with reasonable
care, skill and speed, whether he does them personally or through
independent contractors (*Murly v M'Dermott* (1838) 8 Ad. & El. 138;
Murray v Hall (1849) 7 C.B. 441). Positive action in shoring up the
remaining property is not required if the wall is wholly owned by
the person demolishing it (*Southwark and Vauxhall Water Co. v
Wandsworth Board of Works* [1898] 2 Ch. 603, 612).

If a party wall to which s.38 of the LPA 1925 applies is damaged
by a third party, each adjoining owner can only recover half of the
cost of its repair, as each now only owns half the wall. In so far as
one adjoining owner suffers a withdrawal of support for his half by
damage done to the wall by the other adjoining owner's tenant, his
remedy is against the owner, not the tenant, because the Act places
the burden of the easement upon him (*Apostal v Simmons* [1936] 1
All E.R. 207).

(c) Nuisance

4–24   One neighbour may be liable to the other in nuisance as a result of
disrepair to a party wall. This can effectively create repairing obligations where otherwise none exists. Where dry rot spread through a
party wall, the owner on whose side it started was held liable in
damages, because she should reasonably have appreciated the danger
and there were preventative steps she could reasonably have taken
(*Bradburn v Lindsay* [1983] 2 All E.R. 408). An action in nuisance
was also successful when subsidence caused damage to a party wall,
because the demolition of the house on one side caused the clay soil
to dry out. The nuisance was an interference with the easement of
support (*Brace v South Eastern Regional Housing Association* [1984]
1 E.G.L.R. 144).

No claim for damages for nuisance can be founded on work that
has been authorised under the party wall provisions in the London
Building Acts (*Selby v Whitbread & Co.* [1917] 1 K.B. 736), and
therefore, it is assumed, under the Party Wall etc. Act 1996. However, if damage is caused before the statutory procedure is invoked,

the nuisance continues until remedial work has been completed, even if the a party wall notice has been served in the interim (*Louis v Sadiq* [1997] 1 E.G.L.R. 136).

5 Other shared structures

The statutory provisions relating to party walls extend to other **4–25** shared structures, *e.g.* walls, but are generally confined to those that separate properties in different ownership. There can, however, be some joint responsibility for structures that are wholly within one property but benefit several. Foundations under, or a roof over, a building divided between a number of owners is an example.

The owner of the structure owes a duty of care to the owners of other property affected by it. "The duty is . . . to do that which is reasonable . . . and no more . . . to prevent or minimise the known risk of damage or injury to one's neighbour or to his property." (*Leakey v National Trust for Places of Historic Interest or Natural Beauty* [1980] Q.B. 485 at 524 *per* Megaw L.J.) The duty is "based upon knowledge of the hazard, ability to foresee the consequences of not checking and removing it, and the ability to abate it" (*Goldman v Hargrave* [1967] 1 A.C. 645 at 663 *per* Lord Wilberforce).

However, this is not a duty to do the work. The duty is to contribute to the cost of the work if it is carried out. Accordingly, the owner of the freehold of the upper floors of a building (which was a flying freehold), who neglected roof repairs to the extent that the building was a danger to visitors to the ground floor, was required to contribute to the cost of roof repairs that the owner of the ground floor had carried out (*Abbahall Ltd v Smee* [2003] 1 W.L.R. 1472).

Chapter 5

Hedges

1 Residential property

(a) Adverse effect of high hedges

The Anti-social Behaviour Act 2003 gives the owner or occupier of **5–01**
domestic property a right to complain to the local authority if the
height of a high hedge adversely affects the reasonable enjoyment of
his property. The owner of property that is unoccupied can also
complain, on the basis that a prospective occupier would be affected.
The right to complain does not extend to the effects of the roots of
a high hedge.

If the authority finds the complaint justified, it issues a remedial
notice, stating what immediate action should be taken and what further preventative action is required. There is a right of appeal. It is
an offence not to take the action required by a remedial notice.

(b) Scope of rights

A complaint about a high hedge must relate to its effect on "domes- **5–02**
tic property". This means a dwelling, defined as a building, or part
of one, which is occupied as a separate dwelling, or intended to be
occupied as one. It also covers a garden or yard used and enjoyed
wholly or mainly in connection with a dwelling. The complaint, of
interference with the reasonable enjoyment, need only relate to part
of the property (Anti-social Behaviour Act 2003, s.67).

A "high hedge" for this purpose is one formed wholly or predominantly of a line of at least two evergreen or semi-evergreen trees or
shrubs. The hedge must measure more than two metres above ground
level. There is an exception that may cause difficult arguments: a
hedge is not regarded as forming a barrier to light or access if gaps
significantly affect its overall effect as a barrier at heights over two
metres (Anti-social Behaviour Act 2003, s.66). There is no statutory
definition of evergreen or semi-evergreen. A dictionary definition of
evergreen is, "having green leaves all the year through; opposite to

deciduous" (*Shorter Oxford Dictionary*). "Semi-evergreen" has been defined, "Normally evergreen but losing some or all of its leaves in a cold winter or cold area" (*Hillier's Manual of Trees & Shrubs*, 5th ed., 1981, David & Charles Publishers plc).

Unlike the policy relating to hedgerows on non-residential property, there is no special protection for ancient hedges.

(c) Making a complaint

5–03   A complaint about a high hedge is made to the local authority in whose area the hedge lies. In England, this is the district council, the county council where there is no district, the London borough council or the Common Council of the City of London. In Wales, this is the county council or the county borough council (Anti-social Behaviour Act 2003, s.82). There is no prescribed form. The authority may charge a fee.

Before making a complaint to the authority, the complainant is expected to take all reasonable steps to resolve matters. If the authority considers that he has not done so, it may decide not to proceed with the complaint. It may similarly decide to take no action on a complaint it considers frivolous or vexatious.

In other cases, the authority must take decisions on two matters. The first question is whether the height of the hedge adversely affects the complainant's reasonable enjoyment of the domestic property. If the answer is yes, it must then decide whether, and if so what, remedial action should be taken or what action is needed to prevent recurrence. That action cannot include either lowering the hedge to less than two metres or removing the hedge. If the authority concludes that action should be taken, it issues a remedial notice as soon as practicable. Copies must be sent, with reasons for the decision, to every complainant and to every owner and occupier of the land on which the hedge is growing (Anti-social Behaviour Act 2003, ss.68, 69(3)).

(d) Remedial notices

5–04   The contents of a remedial notice are prescribed. It must state: (i) that a complaint was made about a specified hedge; (ii) that the authority determined that its height adversely affects the complainant's reasonable enjoyment; (iii) the initial action to be taken before the end of the compliance period (a reasonable period specified in the notice); (iv) any preventative action to be taken later; and (v) the fact that failure to comply is an offence and that, in default, the authority may enter to do the work at the defaulter's expense.

5–05   While a remedial notice is in force, it is binding on every person who is for the time being an owner or occupier of the land on which the hedge grows. It is registrable as a local land charge (Anti-social

Behaviour Act 2003, s.69). Failure to register it does not affect its enforceability, but may entitle someone who bought the land to compensation for loss (Local Land Charges Act 1975, s.10).

The authority has power to waive or relax a requirement in a remedial notice that they issued, or may withdraw it (Anti-social Behaviour Act 2003, s.70).

(e) Appeals

Both the complainant and an owner or occupier of the land on which the hedge grows have right of appeal against a local authority decision in relation to a high hedge lies to the Secretary of State, if the hedge is in England, and to the National Assembly for Wales, if the hedge is in Wales. Appeals can relate to: the authority's decision as to whether the height of the hedge adversely affects the complainant's reasonable enjoyment of domestic property and whether, and if so what, action should be taken; the issue of the remedial notice; the withdrawal of the notice; or the waiver or relaxation of its requirements. There is a 28-day time limit for appealing. Regulations are to lay down the procedure (Anti-social Behaviour Act 2003, ss.72, 73).

5–06

(f) Enforcement

An owner or occupier who fails to take action required by a remedial notice is guilty of an offence and subject on summary conviction to a fine of up to £1,000 (standard scale, level 3). Where failure is continuing, the court may also order the defaulter to take steps to secure compliance within a reasonable period; not to comply with that order is also an offence, subject to a fine of up to £1,000 and £20 a day while he continues to fail to comply.

5–07

There are statutory defences: that the accused did everything he could be expected to do to secure compliance; and that he did not know of the notice, was not sent a copy and, when the offence was committed, was not the owner of the land (*i.e.* was entitled to the rack rent or would have been had the land been let), or it was not registered as a local land charge (Anti-social Behaviour Act 2003, s.75).

Where the required action is not taken, the authority may authorise someone to enter the land to do it, and may recover the cost from any owner or occupier of the land (Anti-social Behaviour Act 2003, s.77).

2 Non-residential property

(a) Outline of protection

5–08   An "important" hedge, which is neither within the curtilage of a dwelling-house nor marks its boundary, is protected against being removed (which means uprooted or otherwise destroyed: Environment Act 1995, s.97(8)). Regulations define which hedgerows fall into the "important" category. Preliminary notice must be given to the local planning authority before any substantial hedge is removed, and the authority's consent obtained. In the case of an important hedge, there is a presumption that the authority will issue a hedgerow retention notice, which prohibits removal. It is an offence to remove a hedgerow intentionally or recklessly in contravention of the regulations, or to cause or permit someone else to do so (Hedgerows Regulations 1997).

(b) Hedgerow categories

5–09   The regulations apply to a hedgerow that has a continuous length of at least 20 metres, or is part of one of that length. They also apply to a shorter hedgerow if it meets another hedgerow at both ends, or it is part of a hedgerow that does. Subject to the overall exception of hedgerows on or bounding the curtilage of a dwelling-house, the hedgerows within the scope of the regulations are those growing on, or adjacent to, common land, land used for agriculture, forestry or the breeding or keeping of horses, ponies or donkeys (Hedgerows Regulations 1997, reg.3).

An "important" hedgerow is one in respect of which notice of removal must be given and which has existed for at least 30 years. It must also satisfy at least one of a list of detailed criteria. These relate to: archaeology and history; protected or threatened birds; woody species (Hedgerows Regulations 1997, reg.4, Schs 1–3).

(c) Procedure

5–10   Someone who proposes to remove a hedgerow to which the regulations apply must give notice to the local planning authority (a "hedgerow removal notice"), along with a plan and evidence of the date of planting any stretch planted within the previous 30 years. A form of notice is prescribed, but a notice to substantially the same effect may be used.

The authority has 42 days within which to respond. It may give written notice that the hedgerow may be removed or it may serve a "hedgerow retention notice", which forbids removal. If the authority fails to respond within the time limit, the hedgerow may be removed.

A hedgerow retention notice may only be given in respect of an important hedgerow; but the authority is required to give a notice for such a hedgerow unless it is satisfied that removal is justified for the reasons given in the hedgerow removal notice. There is a right of appeal to the Secretary of State, or in Wales to the National Assembly, against a hedgerow retention notice (Hedgerows Regulations 1997, regs 5, 8, Sch.4).

(d) Work: permitted and forbidden
With the exceptions noted below, it is an offence to remove a   **5–11**
hedgerow intentionally or recklessly in contravention of the regulations, or to cause or permit anyone else to do so. This covers removing any hedgerow to which the regulations apply – not merely an important hedgerow – without giving a hedgerow removal notice and removing an important hedgerow in contravention of a hedgerow retention notice. A person guilty of an offence is liable on summary conviction to a fine of up to £1,000. In addition, the local planning authority have powers to apply to the court for an injunction and may require the freeholder of the land to plant another hedge. There is appeal against a notice to replant to the Secretary of State, or in Wales to the National Assembly (Hedgerows Order 1997, regs 7–9, 11).

There are specified exceptions to the restrictions imposed by the regulations on removing hedgerows. They include: for obtaining access where it is the only way without disproportionate expense or in an emergency, for carrying out development that has planning consent, for drainage, highway and electricity supply purposes, for pest control, for national defence and for proper hedgerow management (Hedgerows Regulations 1997, reg.6).

3 Specific cases

(a) Agricultural holdings
For the duties to repair hedges on an agricultural holding, see under   **5–12**
Duty to Fence.

(b) Inclosure awards
Some inclosure awards imposed on landowners and their successors   **5–13**
in title duties to repair hedges and other boundary features. There was power to do so (*Garnett v Pratt* [1926] Ch. 897). However, a county court judge has held that by analogy with the general rule that a positive covenant is not enforceable against a successor in title of the covenantor (*Austerberry v Oldham Corporation* (1885) 29 Ch.D. 750), a positive obligation imposed by an inclosure award is not enforceable against successors in title of the original owner (*Marlton v Turner* [1998] 3 E.G.L.R. 185 (CC)).

Chapter 6

Duty to Fence

1 No general duty

A landowner is not, simply by reason of his owning property, under **6–01** any obligation to fence his boundaries. There are, however, many cases where there will be such a duty, owed either to certain persons only or to the public at large. The circumstances in which the duty arises are dealt with in detail below. They fall into the following general categories: obligations imposed by agreement; arising by prescription; imposed because of the nature of the land, its situation or the use to which it is put; and special statutory obligations.

Where no obligation exists there can be no liability for damage sustained solely by reason of the lack of a fence. However, where a fence has been erected even though there is no obligation to do so, and it is in a dangerous condition, its owner may be liable for damage resulting from its condition. In appropriate circumstances an action could be maintained in nuisance (where there is detriment to a neighbour's enjoyment of his land: *Harrold v Watney* [1898] 2 Q.B. 320), in negligence (where damage is caused to a person who must have been in the landowner's contemplation and to whom he owes a duty of care: *Terry v Ashton* (1876) 1 Q.B.D. 314), independently of these causes of action if the damage flows naturally from the defective fence (*Firth v Bowling Iron Co.* (1878) 3 C.P.D. 254), or against a landlord who has undertaken to repair (Defective Premises Act 1972, s.4).

2 Obligations on freehold owners

(a) Covenants on conveying freeholds

A covenant to erect and/or maintain a fence contained in a con- **6–02** veyance of freehold property is valid and enforceable between the parties to the conveyance, subject only to the usual limitation period of 12 years from the date of the breach of covenant for suing on a deed. There is, however, no completely satisfactory way to ensure that the obligation to fence will bind every person into whose hands the land comes. Normal conveyancing practice is for the covenantor to obtain an indemnity from his successor in title against loss suffered by him because of a future breach of the covenant, but this does not make the covenant directly enforceable against the new owner. At common law the burden of covenants never passed with the land (*Austerberry v Oldham Corporation* (1885) 29 Ch. D. 750). Equity modified this, but only in the case of restrictive covenants (*Tulk v Moxhay* (1848) 2 Phill. 744). A covenant to fence is a positive covenant and is not therefore affected (*Jones v Price* [1965] 2 Q.B. 618). The benefit of the equitable rules cannot be obtained by phrasing in negative form what is in effect a positive covenant.

A number of possible methods of attaching a fencing obligation to a freehold may be mentioned, although some are rather involved and therefore only likely to be employed in cases where the need is particularly pressing.

The first involves the creation of an estate rentcharge issuing out of the land on which the obligation is to be imposed. This form of rentcharge was introduced by the Rentcharges Act 1977, s.2. The amount of the rentcharge cannot exceed a nominal sum, except to the extent that it pays for maintenance or repairs to the fence. It is not subject to compulsory redemption (s.8(4)).

6–03 The covenant to fence is made one of the covenants entered into with the owner of the rentcharge. A right of re-entry may be reserved to the owner of the rent when it is created, which would be exercisable on breach of covenant, and should be an adequate sanction. The right to exercise it need not be confined to the perpetuity period (Perpetuities and Accumulations Act 1964, s.11(1)). A similar, more limited, provision means that the right does not have to be confined to the perpetuity period in a conveyance of Crown lands by the Crown Estate Commissioners (Crown Estate Act 1961, s.3(8)).

A second way to enforce a fencing covenant is to reserve a right of re-entry in favour of the owner of retained land, when selling part of a holding. A seller does not have to retain a reversion in the land sold in order to do that. The drawback is that unless any default complained of is grave and wilful, it is likely that equitable relief will be granted (*Shiloh Spinners Ltd v Harding* [1973] A.C. 691).

It has also been suggested that the principle of *Halsall v Brizell* [1957] Ch 169, could be employed here: anyone taking advantage of benefits granted by a deed must comply with obligations that it imposes to contribute to costs. That case related, amongst other benefits, to sea walls. Presumably, therefore, there is no difficulty in establishing that a purchaser takes the benefit of a fence or wall, even though the enjoyment of it is essentially passive. However, it is not clear whether the principle extends beyond making an obligation to pay money binding, to enforcing a positive obligation to do work. The last possibility is, instead of conveying the freehold, for the **6–04** seller to grant to the purchaser a lease for at least 300 years at a peppercorn rent and without a proviso for re-entry, so that the buyer can convert it into a fee simple by deed poll under s.153 of the LPA 1925. The obligations created by the covenants in such a lease do not come to an end when the term is enlarged into a freehold, but continue to attach to the freehold (subs. (8)). Accordingly, if the covenant that was required as to fencing was inserted in the lease originally, the obligation would be imposed on successive owners of the freehold. The drawback of this method, which in any event would hardly be suitable for widespread use on the development of an estate, is that it is not clear what measure of damages (if any) would be recoverable in an action for breach of covenant. A landlord normally recovers the amount of the damage to his reversion, but here he has no reversion. It may therefore be that there is no effective sanction to support this obligation.

The Lands Tribunal has held that it has no jurisdiction to discharge a positive covenant to fence, under s.84 of the LPA 1925, because it is a purely personal covenant (*Re Blyth Corporation's Application* (1963) 14 P. & C.R. 56 (L.T.)). If a covenant is satisfactorily made to bind successors in title, it is an open question whether it could be varied. The section refers to a "restriction", and it may be that that would never be apt to include a positive covenant.

Where the freehold of a property was purchased under the provisions for individual leasehold enfranchisement in the Leasehold Reform Act 1967 or collective leasehold enfranchisement under the Leasehold Reform, Housing and Urban Development Act 1993, a management scheme may apply. The terms of the scheme bind the owner of the property for the time being. They can require boundary walls to be maintained (*Mosley v Cooper* [1990] 1 E.G.L.R. 124). New schemes can be introduced, but only with the consent of the Secretary of State. Existing schemes can be varied by applying to a leasehold valuation tribunal (Leasehold Reform, Housing and Urban Development Act 1993, s.75).

(b) Damages on breach of covenant
On a failure to erect a boundary wall in accordance with a covenant **6–05** to do so, the covenantee who owns the adjoining land can recover damages equal to the cost of carrying out the work on his own land. The amount of damages is not limited to the loss of value resulting from the lack of a wall, nor to the cost of erecting the cheapest possible fence in its place (*Radford v De Froberville* [1977] 1 W.L.R. 1262). Damages that amount to the cost of the work when judgment

is given, even if this is greater than it would have been at the date the work should have been done, can be recovered by a plaintiff who could not reasonably have done the work earlier (*Dodd Properties (Kent) Ltd v Canterbury City Council* [1980] 1 W.L.R. 433).

(c) Commonhold units

6–06 A commonhold community statement may, in an appropriate case, impose on unit-holders an obligation to repair and maintain fences on their units (Commonhold and Leasehold Reform Act 2002, s.14(2)). These would be statutory, not contractual, obligations and, without more, would bind all succeeding unit-holders (s.37).

3 Landlord and tenant

(a) Express covenants

6–07 Covenants to erect and/or maintain fences are often found in leases, and they may be by either party. This is certainly one of the matters that a lease should deal with explicitly wherever possible. If there is a covenant to repair the demised premises, it is necessarily a question of construction whether a boundary wall forms part of the demised premises. If it does not, the covenant does not apply to it (*Blundell v Newlands Investment Trust* (1958) 172 E.G. 855).

If the lease is silent, certain obligations will be implied in the case of a tenancy for a term of years, and these may not accord with the parties' wishes. If the tenancy is from year to year or at will, no obligations will attach to either party, which makes the position clear but not satisfactory. The covenants in a "new tenancy" – which is one granted after on or after January 1, 1996, unless it was granted pursuant to an agreement made or an option granted before that date – bind and benefit the landlord and tenant for the time being. Predecessors in title generally cease to be bound by the covenants and cannot enforce them (Landlord and Tenant (Covenants) Act 1995).

In relation to earlier leases, the LPA 1925, ss.141 and 142, provides that the benefits of tenants' covenants and the burden of landlord's covenants, where they have reference to the subject-matter of the lease, run with the reversion, so benefiting and binding whomsoever is in the position of landlord. Covenants that "touch and concern" the land demised run with the land at common law, binding the tenant for the time being, and the benefit of the landlord's covenants runs similarly. Fencing covenants fall within both these definitions, and so remain valid and enforceable against and by the persons then concerned with the land, although one or both of the original parties to the lease have disposed of their interests. There is one possible exception. It may be that a covenant to erect a new fence or boundary wall (rather than merely to repair), in a lease executed prior to 1926, will not bind the tenant's successors in title unless he expressly covenanted for himself and his assigns (*Spence's Case* (1583) 5 Co. Rep. 16a). No difficulty arises in the case of covenants to repair only.

There is no limit to the period for which a fencing covenant in a lease can be effective (the rule against perpetuities not being applicable), so the covenant settles the question of fencing for the duration of the term. Although, formerly, a fencing covenant in a lease could only be enforced by the other party to the lease, a landlord's responsibility for a fence in a dangerous condition is in effect extended to the Defective Premises Act 1972, s.4. Anyone who might reasonably be expected to be affected by defects and who suffers injury or damage, has a remedy against a landlord who knew, or ought to have known, of the defect. A landlord who has reserved a right of entry to repair is, for this purpose only, treated as having covenanted to repair.

(b) Agricultural Holdings
Special provisions apply to the letting of an agricultural holding **6–08** (Agricultural Holdings Act 1986), but not to a farm business tenancy (Agricultural Tenancies Act 1995). Most lettings of agricultural property on or after September 1, 1995 are therefore not affected.

Where these provisions do apply and the terms on which an agricultural holding is let do not expressly deal with fences and walls, certain covenants are implied (Agriculture (Maintenance, Repair and Insurance of Fixed Equipment) Regulations 1973, Sch.). The landlord must execute all repairs and replacements of walls and fences of open and covered yards and garden walls (para.1). The tenant has a duty to repair and leave in good repair, order and condition, various parts of the property, but only to the extent that the matters are not already covered by a landlord's covenant. The tenant's responsibility extends to fences, hedges, field walls, stiles, gates and posts (para.5(1)). Also, he must cut, trim or lay a proper proportion of the hedges each year so as to maintain them in good and sound condition (para.9). These implied covenants are displaced by any written agreement placing responsibility on the other party (*Burden v Hannaford* [1956] 1 Q.B. 143). In determining the extent of the implied obligation, regard must be had to the age, character and condition of the property at the beginning of the tenancy (*Evans v Jones* [1955] 2 Q.B. 58).

In default, the other party may do the work and recover the reasonable cost from the other, although the amount the tenant can recover is limited to the smaller of £2,000 and the annual rent (paras

4(2), 12(2)). Breach of a covenant to maintain fences can also be the foundation of a notice to quit under the Agricultural Holdings Act 1986, Sch.3, Pt I, Case D (*Shepherd v Lomas* [1963] 1 W.L.R. 962).

(c) Short residential lettings

6–09 The Landlord and Tenant Act 1985, s.11, implies repairing covenants on the part of the landlord into almost all short tenancies of residential property. However, it is unlikely that a garden wall or fence would be affected (*Hopwood v Cannock Chase District Council* [1975] 1 W.L.R. 373).

(d) Covenants implied at common law

6–10 Apart from express provisions in the lease and the statutory provisions relating to agricultural holdings, the occupier of premises let for a term of years is liable to repair fences, but tenants from year to year or at will are not. This is because only tenants for years are liable for permissive waste. The landlord can maintain an action against the tenant where the repairs are not carried out, on the ground of damage to his inheritance (*Cheetham v Hampson* (1791) 4 Term Rep. 318), and if the fences fall down by reason of excavations in breach of covenant, a mandatory injunction may be granted to renew them (*Newton v Nock* (1880) 43 L.T. 197). Provided the landlord has not undertaken to repair the fences and (unless the tenant has agreed to put them in good repair) they were not dilapidated at the start of the term, the occupier is liable to any third party injured because of the want of repair.

For the performance of his obligations the occupier is entitled to fell timber (*i.e.* oak, ash and elm over 20 years old, and possibly other wood by local custom), the felling of which is generally waste. The use is known as "estovers", but only felling for immediate fencing requirements is permitted.

(e) Compensation

6–11 Compensation is payable to the outgoing tenant of an agricultural holding in respect of improvements taking the form of the making or removal of permanent fences (Agricultural Holdings Act 1986, Schs 7, 8). If the improvement was begun before March 1, 1948 (an "old improvement"), the landlord's consent must have been obtained. For later improvements (a "new improvement"), the tenant must either have the landlord's consent or the Minister's approval. A tenant who is aggrieved by his landlord withholding consent may apply to the Agricultural Land Tribunal (s.67(3)). The amount of compensation for an old improvement is such sum as fairly represents its value to an incoming tenant (Sch.9, Pt I, para.2(1)). For a new improvement, compensation equals the increase in the value of the holding attributable to the improvement, having regard to the character and situation of the holding and the average requirements of tenants reasonably skilled in husbandry (s.66(1)).

The tenant under a farm business tenancy is also entitled to compensation when he quits for improvements that he made at his own expense with his landlord's consent (Agricultural Tenancies Act 1995, s.17). The amount of it equals the increase in the value of the property at the end of the tenancy attributable to the improvement (s.20).

4 Fencing easements

A landowner may acquire an easement for his neighbour to fence the **6–12** boundary between their properties, or to maintain a hedge along it (*Jones v Price* [1965] 2 Q.B. 618). The duty arises when the work is not done for the benefit of the person doing it, but rather for his neighbour's benefit (*Hudson v Tabor* (1877) 2 Q.B.D. 290, 292 *per* Lord Coleridge C.J.).

This is not an easement that is covered by the Prescription Act 1832, so title to the right must be made in other ways. This could be *e.g.* under the LPA 1925, s.62 on a conveyance by the former owner of the dominant and servient tenements (*Crow v Wood* [1971] 1 Q.B. 77), or by prescription at common law. The latter theoretically involves proof that the right dates back to the limit of legal memory, 1189. In practice, a long period of exercise of the right is accepted if there is no definite proof that the right previously did not exist. Alternatively, the court may apply the doctrine of the lost modern grant: *i.e.* the presumption that the duty must have been imposed by a document now lost. In either case proof of 20 or 30 years' undisputed exercise of the right is likely to succeed in the absence of evidence to the contrary. A right is normally established by proof that the owner of the servient tenement and his predecessors in title have been in the habit of carrying out all necessary repairs to the fence at their own expense, and doing so on receiving notice to do so from the owner of the dominant tenement and his predecessors.

It is interesting to contrast two cases. Evidence that the owners of one piece of land had repaired a certain fence for 50 years was held insufficient to establish an easement, in the absence of any evidence that they did so as a result of an obligation (*Hilton v Ankesson* (1872) 27 L.T. 519). On the other hand, evidence that a fence had been repaired by one party and his predecessors for 40 years was held sufficient, when combined with the fact that for the last 19 years they had done so on notice from those claiming the benefit of the easement (*Lawrence v Jenkins* (1873) L.R. 8 Q.B. 274).

6–13   The landowner subject to the obligation is not entitled to notice of the want of repair. He is liable for all resulting damage, including escape of his neighbour's cattle, even though he was ignorant of the need for repair. He is not liable for the results of damage to the fence by act of God or *vis major*. Where the servient tenement is let, the action in cases of non-repair is against the tenant, not the landlord (*Lawrence v Jenkins* (1873) L.R. 8 Q.B. 274).

No obligation can arise by prescription whereby one owner has to maintain a wall merely to protect his neighbour's building against penetration of the weather. This proposition derives from a decision that this is not a right that can constitute an easement (*Phipps v Pears* [1965] 1 Q.B. 76). However, this must be doubtful in the light of the finding "that it would be right to hold that [the neighbour withdrawing support] was under a duty . . . to take reasonable steps to provide weatherproofing" (*Rees v Skerrett* [2001] 3 E.G.L.R. 1 at [37] *per* Lloyd J.). If a wall is laid bare in the course of demolition, the local authority may require that the demolisher make it weatherproof (Public Health Act 1961, s.29). The neighbouring owner may also be able to exercise rights under the Party Wall etc. Act 1996.

A prescriptive obligation to fence comes to an end if the dominant and servient tenements come into the same ownership, in such a way that the estate for which each is held is identical (*Canham v Fisk* (1831) 2 C. & J. 126).

5 Obligations arising from particular circumstances

(a) Highway and land adjoining

6–14   At common law there was no duty to fence a boundary with a highway.* This formerly meant that there was no liability for damage caused by animals straying on to the road. Now, however, the normal rules apply (Animals Act 1971, s.8). There are exceptions. Merely placing animals on unfenced land does not, without more, constitute a breach of duty if the person had the right to place animals on the land and that land is common land, is situated in an area where fencing is not customary, or is a town or village green. The keeper of any horses, cattle, sheep, goats or swine – the person in whose possession they are – commits an offence if they stray onto the highway, except where it passes over common, waste or unenclosed ground (Highways Act 1980, s.155).

---

* In fact from the reign of Edward I to that of George III it was forbidden to maintain a dyke, tree or bush "whereby a man may work to do hurt" within 200 feet of either side of a highway, as a protection against highwaymen, rogues and vagabonds (*Searle v Wallbank* [1947] A.C. 341, 347–8).

The Highways Act 1980, s.165, imposes an obligation upon the owner of land adjoining a street (which includes *inter alia* a highway, lane, footpath or passage, whether a thoroughfare or not) adequately to fence anything thereon that is a source of danger to persons using the street (as, for example, a building in the course of demolition). This is enforced by the local authority serving on the owner notice to execute the necessary works and, subject to an appeal to the magistrates' court, on his failure to comply the authority may carry out the work at the owner's expense. Where the only source of danger is the difference in level between the road and the adjoining land, the owner cannot be compelled to fence because the danger does not exist in or on his land (*Myers v Harrow Corporation* [1962] 2 Q.B. 442). There are also statutory obligations to fence certain objects of danger within certain distances of a road, such as steam engines, windmills and dangerous quarries.

Where a fence has been erected adjoining a highway, liability will arise if it is allowed to fall into such a state of dilapidation that it is a nuisance, and any person using the highway is injured as a natural result (*Harrold v Watney* [1898] 2 Q.B. 32)).

Where the land adjoining a highway is fenced with barbed wire, or   **6–15**
the fence contains barbed wire, which is a nuisance to the highway (*i.e.* if it is likely to be injurious to persons or animals lawfully using the highway), the highway authority can serve a notice on the occupier to abate the nuisance within a specified time (not less than one month nor more than six months) (Highways Act 1980, s.164). If the highway authority is itself the occupier any ratepayer can initiate similar action.

A fence that is dangerous to persons lawfully using the highway can also lead to a civil action for nuisance. Actions have been brought successfully where the injury was caused by wire (*Stewart v Wright* (1893) 9 T.L.R. 480) and spikes (*Morrison v Sheffield Corporation* [1917] 2 K.B. 866).

Where a hedge, tree or shrub overhangs any road or footpath to which the public has access and endangers, obstructs or interferes with the passage or view of vehicle drivers or pedestrians or the light from a public lamp, the appropriate authority may require it to be lopped within 14 days or (subject to an appeal to the magistrates' court) do it themselves at the owner's or occupier's expense (Highways Act 1980, s.154). On the other hand, where a hedge is within the boundaries of the highway and, because of the lack of routine maintenance, it is so overgrown that it obstructs the highway, the highway authority has a duty to cut it back (Highways Act 1980, s.41; *Worcestershire County Council v Newman* [1974] 1 W.L.R. 938, construing Highways Act 1959, s.59).

No door, gate or bar on any premises may open outwards on a street, except in the case of a public building with the consent of the local authority and the highway authority. An owner may be given eight days in which to alter an offending door (Highways Act 1980, s.153).

6–16   It is an offence to erect a fence or plant a hedge in a highway that consists of or comprises a carriageway for vehicles (Highways Act 1980, s.138). A person interested in land adjoining or near a highway may enter into an agreement with the highway authority restricting or regulating the use of the land, and in particular what grows on it. The agreement is registrable as a local land charge (Highways Act 1980, s.253).

Vaults, arches and cellars under streets must be kept in good repair. In default, the local authority may do necessary work and recover the expense (Highways Act 1980, s.180(6), (7)). A person injured has no action against a defaulter (*Scott v Green & Sons* [1969] 1 W.L.R. 301).

A highway authority, may, and in some circumstances must, fence the highway. If a fence protecting highway users from a dangerous drop, or a stream, is part of the highway – which is a question of fact as to whether it is built on land originally dedicated or acquired for the highway – it is repairable with the highway (*R. v Whitney* (1835) 7 C. & P. 208). Where the authority, or its predecessors in title, have fenced a dangerous place, it may be liable for damage resulting from removal of the fence (*Whyler v Bingham Rural Council* [1901] 1 K.B. 45). A highway authority may erect and maintain a fence to prevent access to a road. This power may not, however, be exercised in such a way as to interfere with a gate used for agricultural purposes, a public right of way, or a means of access to the road for which planning permission has been granted or for which it was not needed because it existed on July 1, 1948 and did not contravene the earlier legislation (Highways Act 1980, s.80). In any area of the countryside where walls of a particular construction are a feature, the highway authority's powers and duties relating to fences can apply to walls of that construction (Wildlife and Countryside Act 1981, s.72(12)). A special road authority may stop up private means of access to special roads (*e.g.* motorways) and provide alternative means of access to adjoining premises (1980 Act, s.125).

(b) Land accessible to the public
6–17   A local authority has power to require works, which may include fencing, to remove the danger from an excavation on land accessible to the public from a highway, or on a place of public resort. In default, or where the authority does not know the identity of the

owner or occupier of the land, it must carry out the work required
(Local Government (Miscellaneous Provisions) Act 1976, s.25).

(c) Land adjoining a common

An owner of land adjoining a common may, by prescription, become
liable to fence his property against the beasts grazing on the common, although only with a fence capable of keeping out the type that
usually graze there (*Coaker v Willcocks* [1911] 2 K.B. 124). Breach of
such an obligation gives rise to at least a claim for nominal damages
by the owner of cattle that stray off the common (*Egerton v Harding*
[1975] Q.B. 62). **6–18**

(d) Animals

The owner of livestock (cattle, horses, asses, mules, hinnies, sheep,
pigs, goats, poultry, deer not in the wild state, and captive pheasants,
partridges and grouse) is liable for any damage to land or property
that it causes when it strays on to someone else's land (Animals Act
1971, s.4). The owner is also liable for the cost of maintaining the
livestock before it is restored to him. For this purpose, the person
who has possession of the livestock is liable as owner. There is no
liability where the animals stray from the highway, provided their
presence there was a lawful use of the highway (s.5(5)). **6–19**

The fact that the land on to which the animals strayed was not
fenced is not of itself a defence. But the livestock owner is not liable
if he can establish that the animals would not have strayed but for a
breach of a duty to fence by someone interested in the land (s.5(6)).
The duty to fence does not have to be owed to the livestock owner.
It could be an obligation attached to the freehold or a covenant in a
lease. (This accordingly reverses the decision in *Holgate v Bleazard*
[1917] 1 K.B. 443, where the tenant of a farm recovered damages for
injuries to a colt on his land caused by horses that strayed onto his
land because he had failed to comply with a lease covenant to maintain the boundary fence.)

A landowner has a duty of care to users of an adjoining highway
to prevent stock known to be on the land from straying. But when a
heifer strayed from land let on a grass keep agreement and caused an
accident, the landowner was not liable because there was no evidence
that he knew the fencing to be inadequate (*Hoskin v Rogers* (1985)
The Times, January 25).

If any horses, cattle, sheep, goats or swine are found straying or
lying on or at the side of the highway, their keeper (the person in
whose possession they are) is liable to a fine (Highways Act 1980,
s.155). This does not apply where the highway crosses common, waste
or unenclosed land, and is without prejudice to any right of pasture
on the side of the highway. However, there was an offence where a cow

strayed from common land onto a road and went 300 yards along the road away from the common, where a car collided with it (*Rees v Morgan* (1960) *The Times*, February 14).

(e) Dangerous objects and operations

6–20 The occupier of land used for dangerous operations or for the storage of dangerous objects must consider fencing obligations from two points of view: to prevent the escape from his land of dangerous things, or objects made dangerous by the activities on his land, and to prevent the entry of persons who are likely to be harmed there.

The rule in *Rylands v Fletcher* (1868) L.R. 3 H.L. 330, imposes upon the occupier of land a strict liability for the results of the escape from that land of dangerous objects normally there, or accumulated there in unnatural quantities. No negligence is necessary. Act of God, statutory authority, act of a third party and consent or default of the injured party are defences.

Apart from this, an occupier may be liable under the general law of negligence for the results of the escape of something from his land, such as a golf ball (*Castle v St Augustine's Links* (1922) 38 T.L.R. 615), or a football (*Hilder v Associated Portland Cement Manufacturers Ltd* [1961] 1 W.L.R. 1434). This is not an absolute liability; it depends upon whether he could reasonably have foreseen what happened, which is a question of fact. The number of times similar things have happened before and the cost of preventing it are relevant (*Bolton v Stone* [1951] A.C. 850).

The Occupiers' Liability Act 1957, s.2, imposes upon the occupier of premises the duty to take such care as in all the circumstances of the case is reasonable to see that a visitor will be reasonably safe using the premises for the purpose for which he has been invited or permitted to be there. As permission to enter will be assumed in cases where people habitually use the premises, although not expressly authorised, the obligation will probably only be discharged by the erection and maintenance of fences to exclude them where the premises are themselves inherently dangerous (such as a deep gravel pit). The Act expressly states as an example that, in assessing whether a degree of care is reasonable in any case, consideration should be given to the fact that children are less careful than adults, and accordingly it may be more necessary to fence against them. Where premises are occupied for business purposes, the occupier cannot exclude his liability for breach of this common duty of care in so far as it results in death or personal injury, and can only do so in the case of other loss if in all the circumstances it is reasonable (Unfair Contract Terms Act 1977, ss.1, 2).

6 Statutory obligations

(a) Railways
The Railways Clauses Consolidation Act 1845, s.68, imposed upon   **6–21**
railway companies acquiring land compulsorily the obligation to
fence it in perpetuity as part of the accommodation works. This duty
persists and now falls on Railtrack plc or the Strategic Rail Authority (Railways Act 1993, Transport Act 2000). It even continues after
the land has ceased to be used for railway purposes (*R. Walker & Son
v British Railways Board* [1984] 1 W.L.R. 805).
   The extent of the duty to fence is limited. The obligation is to
mark the limit of railway property. There is no general duty to fence
in such a way as to exclude adult or child trespassers (*Proffitt v
British Railways Board* (1985) *The Times*, February 4).
   The original acquiring companies were, however, empowered to
pay compensation in return for a release from their fencing obligations where the vendor agreed. Many such releases were in fact
effected. It is not always clear today, however, whether or not this
happened in respect of any particular stretch of line, because the
railways do still maintain some fences where they are not obliged to.
Normally, where a release was granted, it was stated in the conveyance of the land to the railway company, but even if a duplicate
or counterpart conveyance was executed then, it may be that because
of the lapse of time, no record of the release now appears on the
title. It is therefore wise to make enquiries about this when buying or
taking a lease of land bordering a railway.
   Anyone using an accommodation way across a railway must close
and fasten any gate, or lower any barrier, as soon as he has driven
over or taken animals across. Failure to do so is an offence (Railway
Clauses Consolidation Act 1845, s.75; Transport and Works Act
1992, s.49).

(b) Parsonages
Church of England incumbents are required, by order of the Par-   **6–22**
sonages Board or the Diocesan Board of Finance, to carry out
repairs, specified by the diocesan surveyor, to the walls, fences and
gates of the parsonage house and any former parsonage house while
vested in them (Repair of Benefice Buildings Measure 1972, ss.2–6;
Endowments and Glebe Measure 1976, s.33).

(c) Churchyards and burial grounds
The parochial church council or the burial board, as the case may be,   **6–23**
must maintain the boundary walls and fences of a disused churchyard or burial ground. Upon their certifying the cost of the repairs,
they are entitled to repayment from the general rates, except where

there is another fund legally chargeable with the expense (Burial Act 1855, s.18; Parochial Church Councils (Powers) Measure 1921; Rating and Valuation Act 1925, s.4). A cemetery company is bound to maintain the boundary walls and fences of a cemetery in good repair and, in the absence of special provisions, these must be substantial walls or iron railings at least eight feet high (Cemeteries Clauses Act 1847).

(d) Disused mines

6–24   The owner of an abandoned mine, or one that has not been worked for 12 months, must fence it, to prevent injury to persons or animals falling down the shaft (Mines and Quarries Act 1954, s.151).

(e) Local legislation

6–25   In some areas, local authorities have powers under local Acts to oblige owners to repair boundary walls and fences. In Manchester, *e.g.*, a district council can require the repair, replacement or renewal of a party or boundary wall or fence of any house, if it has collapsed, is in danger of collapsing, or is in a ruinous or dilapidated condition (Greater Manchester Act 1981, s.43(1)).

7 Obligation not to fence

(a) Covenants not to fence

6–26   Some conveyances and leases contain covenants not to fence specified boundaries. This is common enough on modern housing estates laid out with open plan front gardens. A mandatory injunction is the appropriate remedy for the removal of a fence erected in contravention of such a covenant, but it will not be issued in every case (*Shepherd Homes Ltd v Sandham* [1971] Ch. 340). However, there is no need to show that the plaintiff has suffered loss, or that the defendant has made a profit, before a mandatory injunction will be issued (*Harlow Development Corporation v Myers* [1979] 1 E.G.L.R. 143 (CC).

6–27   *(b) Commons*

Erecting a fence that prevents or impedes access to common land is forbidden unless it has ministerial approval, or in Wales the approval of the National Assembly (Law of Property Act 1925, s.194). Where a common is owned by the National Trust, it has power to erect a fence (National Trust Act 1971, s.23), but, again, if access is impeded it must have ministerial approval (*National Trust v Ashbrook* [1997] 4 All E.R. 76).

Chapter 7

Rights of Entry

1 Common law position

There is no general right to enter neighbouring property to repair a   **7–01**
boundary fence or a flank wall, even if that is the most convenient,
or even the only practicable, means of doing it (*Kwiatkowski v Cox*
[1970] E.G.D. 9). An owner who enters to repair without authority
can be restrained by injunction (*John Trenberth Ltd v National
Westminster Bank Ltd* (1969) 39 P. & C.R. 104).

There are, however, a number of ways in which a landowner may
be authorised to enter to do repairs.

(a) Express agreement

The owner of the land which the fence owner needs to enter can of   **7–02**
course give permission. That consent may be for a single occasion,
for a limited period or permanent. If it is to bind the successors in
title of the person granting permission it will need to constitute an
easement. Should the grant not take effect as a legal easement –
because it is not granted in fee simple or for a term of years absolute
or it is not granted by deed – and yet it is still a right of the same
nature, it should be protected by registration. It can be registered as
an equitable easement, land charge class D(iii), or protected on the
land register by a notice.

A landlord who covenants in a lease to repair fences on the
demised premises has an implied right of entry to do the work (*Saner
v Bilton* (1878) 7 Ch. D. 815). This may also apply even if the landlord has not undertaken an obligation to repair, but both parties
expect him to do the work (*Mint v Good* [1951] 1 K.B. 517).

If it was the tenant who covenanted to repair, and he does not, the
landlord can only enter the property to make good the default if he
expressly reserved the right to do so (*Regional Properties Ltd v City
of London Real Property Co. Ltd; Sedgwick Forbes Bland Payne
Group Ltd v Regional Properties Ltd* [1981] 1 E.G.L.R. 33).

(b) Implied authority

7–03   A right of access can arise by prescription, even if that has the effect of placing a restriction on the use to which the neighbour can put the strip of land (*Ward v Kirkland* [1967] Ch. 194).

In the same case it was suggested, although somewhat tentatively, that the doctrine that a person may not derogate from his grant, would also apply. So, where part of a property is sold off, including a wall on the boundary common to the seller and buyer, the buyer may enter the retained land to maintain his property. It may not be necessary to rely on that doctrine, because the LPA 1925, s.62, implying the general words into a conveyance, will have the effect of vesting a right of entry in the buyer.

(c) Shared facilities

7–04   Where one person's property is placed at risk by a neighbouring property owner's neglect, and the neighbouring owner is under no duty to do repairs, the first owner can obtain an injunction giving him the right to enter to do the work (*Abbahall Ltd v Smee* [2003] 1 W.L.R. 1472 at 1482).

(d) Party walls

7–05   As has already been mentioned, one joint owner of a party wall has the right to enter his neighbour's property to carry out repairs and there are statutory rights under the Party Wall etc. Act 1996.

2 Statutory rights

(a) Access to neighbouring land

7–06   The provisions of the Access to Neighbouring Land Act 1992 are dealt with separately below.

(b) Landlord and tenant: residential property

7–07   A number of statutes regulating particular types of residential tenancy give the landlord a right of entry to do the repairs he is entitled to do. It is to be noted that that authority goes beyond merely the repairs that a statute obliges the landlord to do, and indeed beyond the work he covenants to do. This condition applies to assured tenancies (Housing Act 1988, s.16), protected tenancies (Rent Act 1977, s.148) and statutory tenancies of agricultural tied accommodation (Rent (Agriculture) Act 1976, Sch.5, para.8).

(c) Party Wall etc. Act 1996

7–08   The rights of entry conferred by this Act have been dealt with earlier.

(d) Statutory nuisance

A wall in imminent danger of collapse may constitute a public nuisance (*e.g. Kirklees Metropolitan Borough Council v Field* [1997] E.G.C.S. 151). In such a case, the local authority has a power to enter on the land to inspect or to carry out repairs (Environmental Protection Act 1990, Sch.3, para.2).

7–09

(e) High hedges

In connection with the procedure for the owner or occupier of domestic property to complain about the adverse effect that a high hedge has on his reasonable enjoyment of the property, the local authority may authorise a person to enter the land on which the hedge grows. This applies both to inspection and investigation before a remedial notice has been issued and to doing required work if the owner or occupier defaults (Anti-social Behaviour Act 2003, ss.74, 77).

7–09.1

(f) Non-residential hedgerows

A person authorised by a local planning authority has a right of entry on land for purposes connected with the control of removal of hedges. This does not extend to doing work (Hedgerows Regulations 1997, regs 12–14).

7–10

3 Access to Neighbouring Land Act 1992

(a) General scheme

The object of the 1992 Act is to provide a way in which a landowner who lacks authority to enter neighbouring land to do necessary work to his own property can obtain that authority. It also extends to authorising work on a party wall (*Dean v Walker* (1996) 73 P. & C.R. 366). In the absence of agreement, he may apply to court for an access order, which will permit him to enter. An agreement purporting to exclude or restrict someone's right to apply for an access order is void (s.4(4)).

7–11

The Act does not extend to authorising entry onto a highway for the purpose of doing works (s.8(3): definition of "land"), nor to entry onto Crown land, as the Act is not stated to bind the Crown.

The right to apply for an order is deliberately confined to those who do not have the neighbour's consent (s.1(1)). In a case where consent has already been given, but the landowner does not wish to avail himself of it – perhaps because he is required to make a payment, or because it requires work to be done in a particular way that is not the most convenient – there is no additional statutory right.

The landowner must also justify the need for an order. The work must be "reasonably necessary for the preservation" of all or part of

7–12

his property, and it has to be impossible or substantially more difficult to carry out without going on the neighbouring land (s.1(2)). In addition, there is an overall prohibition on making an order if it would be unreasonable, having regard to the degree of interference or disturbance with the use or enjoyment of the neighbouring land, or the hardship suffered by the occupier (s.1(3)).

The way in which the order achieves its purpose is to require the respondent, so far as he has the power, to permit the applicant and those whom he may reasonably authorise ("his associates") to enter and do the work that it authorises. They can, unless the order modifies these rights, take reasonably necessary materials, plant and equipment onto the neighbouring land, leave them there for the period during which the work is permitted, removing them at the end of that time (s.3(1), (2), (7)).

Merely preventing the respondent to the applicant's action from taking action for trespass or nuisance against the applicant begs the question who is entitled to object to the work being done. There may, of course, be more than one person with rights in the neighbouring property that allow him to do so, e.g. the freeholder, the leaseholder and the person entitled to a right of way. It is the applicant who must decide with whose consent he needs to dispense by obtaining an order. Careful enquiries should be made before applying for an order to ensure that all who legitimately oppose the entry are made respondents. If it is not reasonably possible to ascertain the identity of the person who should be made respondent, the applicant may be able to apply for an order against that person by description rather than name. There is power to make rules of court to that effect (s.4(3)), but no rules have yet been made.

(b) Work to be done

7–13 The statutory scheme is confined to work reasonably necessary to preserve all or part of the property in question (s.1(2)).

This is amplified by a provision which automatically covers what the Act calls "basic preservation works" that it is reasonably necessary to carry out. These basic preservation works include a number of items relevant here: first, the maintenance, repair or renewal of any part of a building or other structure, which would cover boundary walls and fences; secondly, the treatment, cutting back, felling, removal or replacement of any hedge, tree or shrub, when damaged, diseased, dangerous, insecurely rooted or dead, or becoming so; and thirdly, filling in or clearing a ditch (s.1(4)).

Work is not necessarily ruled out because it involves either making an alteration, adjustment or improvement or demolition. The court must, in such a case, consider it fair and reasonable in all the circumstances (s.1(5)). Consequential work can be authorised, and that includes inspection to ascertain whether work is needed, doing surveys and plotting the position of services (s.1(6), (7)).

(c) Application for an order
An application for an access order is to be started in the county court   **7–14**
(s.7; for procedure, see CPR Pt 56 PD, para.11).
To make an access order, the court must be satisfied on three
points (subs (1)–(3)):

(1) The applicant does not already have the necessary consent to
     enter the adjoining land for that purpose.

(2) The work cannot be carried out without entering the other
     land, or that would make it substantially more difficult.

(3) The entry on the land will not, to a degree that would make it
     unreasonable to make the order, interfere with or disturb anyone's use or enjoyment of the adjoining land or cause anyone
     who occupies all or part of it to suffer hardship. These considerations are not merely confined to the respondent to the
     court application. This consideration overrides condition (2).

(d) Terms of order
There are three matters which an access order has to specify (s.2(1)).   **7–15**
It must state what works the applicant may carry out from the neighbouring property, onto what part of the property he is authorised to
enter and when and for how long entry is allowed. The order also
places three positive duties on the applicant (s.3(3)). First, he must
ensure that waste is removed from the neighbouring land forthwith.
Secondly, he must, so far as reasonably practicable, make that land
good before the period during which entry is authorised expires.
Finally, he has to indemnify the respondent against damage to the
land or to goods which would not have been caused had the order
not been made.
Conditions can be placed on the order, to avoid or restrict loss,
damage, injury, inconvenience or loss or privacy. In particular, there
can be conditions about the way the work is to be done, the days and
time of the work, who may enter, and the precautions to be taken
(s.2(2), (3)). The order may restrict applicant's rights to take materials, plant and equipment on the neighbouring land (s.3(4)).
The court can also require the applicant to reimburse expenses
that the respondent incurs in connection with the application and
that cannot otherwise be recovered as costs. It can also order the
applicant to give security for payment of compensation (see below)
or of sums under the indemnity he gives for damage caused (s.2(9)).

(e) Compensation

7–16 Where an access order is made to permit work on non-residential land, the applicant can be required to pay the respondent compensation (s.2(5)–(8)). It is the nature of the applicant's property that governs whether compensation is payable, not the nature of the land on which he goes to do the work. For this purpose, residential land is property that is a dwelling, or part of one, and other parts of a building used mainly with any dwelling in it. It extends to a garden, yard, private garage or outbuilding used or enjoyed wholly or mainly with a dwelling.

The amount of compensation is what is fair and reasonable having regard to two factors:

(1) The financial benefit to the applicant and connected person (the owner of any estate or interest in the property on which the work is to be done, or any right over it, any occupier of that property or anyone whom the applicant can reasonably permit to enter for the work authorised by the order). This is whichever is the greater of: either the amount by which the value of the applicant's land is likely to rise as a result of doing the work, less the cost of the work; or the difference in the cost of work if done without entering the neighbouring property and the cost with the benefit of the access order.

(2) The degree of inconvenience which the entry is likely to cause to the respondent or others.

(f) Successors in title

7–17 The benefit of an access order belongs only to the applicant; it does not extend to the owners of other interests in the property, nor to the applicant's successors in title.

On the other hand, an order may be binding on the respondent's successors, *i.e.* later owners of the neighbouring land. To the extent that the court considers it just and equitable, they have power to enforce the order and its terms and conditions, so *e.g.* a later owner may claim compensation (s.4(2)).

In principle, an order binds the respondent's successors and anyone deriving title under him whose estate or interest was created after the order was made (s.4(1)). The class of people whom the order affects would therefore include those who buy and inherit the land from the respondent and tenants under leases that he created after the date of the order. However, the extent to which successors in title are bound is affected by the rules relating to registration.

7–18 An application for an access order comes into the category of pending land action and an order when made is registrable in the register of writs and orders affecting land (Land Charges Act 1972, ss. 5(1)(*a*), 6(1)(*a*); 1992 Act, s.5(1), (6)). In the case of registered land, an application and an order may be protected by the registration of a notice (Land Registration Act 2002, s.34(1); Land Registration Rules 2003, r.172; 1992 Act, s.5(2), (5)).

If an application for an order is not registered and the neighbouring land is sold, the effect on the buyer varies depending upon whether the title is registered. If it is, the application is postponed to the interest acquired by the buyer (Land Registration Act 2002, s.29). In the case of unregistered land, a buyer only takes free from an unregistered application if he does not know of it (Land Charges Act 1972, s.5(7)). Once an order has been made, it must be registered if it is to bind a buyer (1925 Act, s.59(6); 1972 Act s.6(4)).

(g) Agreements instead of orders
Neighbours will normally wish to negotiate access to do work from adjoining property rather than having to obtain a court order, even if the negotiations are conducted in the shadow of the Act. However, it is open to question whether the parties can effectively obtain the same benefits for themselves without resort to the court.   **7–19**

A property owner can, of course, at any time agree that his neighbour may enter his land for a specified purpose either free or on terms. But that is an arrangement between those particular parties. An access order confers two important further benefits: first, provided it is registered, it will bind future owners of the neighbouring land; and secondly, those future owners will be able to enforce the positive obligations which bind the applicant, *e.g.* reinstatement and the payment of compensation. It should be possible in drafting the agreement to allow the neighbour's successors in title to enforce it, but it will not always be possible to guarantee that those successors are bound by the agreement.

If the rights created by an agreement are to be made binding on the neighbouring owner's successor, they will have to create an interest known to the law and be capable of protection on the register. They may constitute an equitable easement or the agreement may be an estate contract ("a contract . . . to convey or create a legal estate": Land Charges Act 1972, s.2(4)(iv)), in which case there is no problem. But the terms of the agreement may not allow it to fall within either of these categories, in which case successors may well not be bound.

Those who are seeking rights of entry to repair, and their advisers, may therefore consider that, except in minor cases where there will be no delay, applying for a formal access order offers definite advantages.

(h) Impact of the Act on other provisions

7–20   In one application to a leasehold valuation tribunal to approve the terms of a management scheme for a central London estate, for the purposes of leasehold enfranchisement (Leasehold Reform, Housing and Urban Development Act 1993, s.70), the proposed scheme included rights of entry when necessary to repair neighbouring property. Objectors argued that the 1992 Act rendered that unnecessary. However, the scheme was approved with that provision included (*Re Grosvenor Estate (Mayfair) London's Application* [1995] 2 E.G.L.R. 201 (LVT)). Presumably, this recognised that the statutory rights – involving an application to court each time they are to be exercised, and being subject to a discretion as to the reasonableness of making an order – are less satisfactory for the "dominant" landowner than an absolute entitlement to enter.

Chapter 8

Miscellaneous

1 Planning

The erection of walls and fences is an operation that is within the **8–01** definition of development in the Town and Country Planning Act 1990, s.55, and accordingly permission is necessary before it can lawfully be done. General permission is, however, given for the erection of certain fences, etc., by the Town and Country Planning (General Permitted Development) Order 1995. This deems permission to have been given for the erection or alteration of certain gates, fences, walls and other means of inclosure that are not within the curtilage of a listed building or on its boundary. The deemed permission relates to structures of a limited height. They are permitted if they do not exceed whichever is greater of their previous height and one metre when adjacent to a highway used by vehicles, or two metres in other cases. There seems to be no authority as to how far back from the road a side wall has to be before it can be said not to be adjacent to the road. An inspector hearing an appeal against an enforcement notice decided that a fence 38 cm back from a highway abutted it (the earlier expression) (T/APP/5337/C/82/1995/G4).

To be covered by this provision, the wall must serve to enclose property. But if, in addition, it has another purpose (*e.g.* retaining banked soil) that does not prevent the consent from applying (*Prengate Properties Ltd v Secretary of State for the Environment* (1973) 25 P. & C.R. 311).

The permission granted by the Order may be removed in certain cases by a direction of the local planning authority confirmed by the Secretary of State. One of the agreed standard enquiries to accompany local land charges searches to all local authorities asks whether such a direction applies to the property in question. A condition imposed on a planning consent can also have the effect of negating the general permission.

8–02   A fence may in some circumstances be erected as a wind-break for agricultural purposes. It is then permitted agricultural development (*Cotswold District Council v Secretary of State for the Environment* (1993) E.G.C.S. 49). A requirement that specified trees be fenced for protection may be validly imposed as a condition attached to a planning permission (*e.g. Leisure Great Britain plc v Isle of Wight Council* (1999) 80 P. & C.R. 370).

Erecting a parapet wall around a flat roof over a house extension constitutes the enlargement of the house requiring permission, unless it is within the limits permitted by the Order (*Richmond London Borough Council v Secretary of State for the Environment* [1991] E.G.C.S. 37).

The formation or laying out of means of access to highway is also an operation that requires planning permission. This applies to access, whether private or public, for vehicles or pedestrians. It extends to all streets, but the Order gives an automatic consent where the road is not a classified one and the work is required in connection with development for which permission has been given.

2 Settled land

(a) Duty to fence

8–03   In the absence of a direction in the trust instrument, a tenant for life is not bound, by virtue of his position as such, to erect or repair fences on the boundaries of the settled property (*Re Cartwright* (1889) 41 Ch. D. 532; *Woodhouse v Walker* (1880) 5 Q.B.D. 404), except where the settled land is leasehold and the lease casts the obligation on the tenant. As occupier of the property, however, he has the normal obligations under the general law. On the other hand, unless the trust instrument expressly gives him an interest "without impeachment of waste" the tenant for life is liable for "voluntary waste", which would include the positive action of destroying a boundary fence. Damages are recoverable for the injury done by an act of waste, and any person interested under the settlement may apply for an injunction to prevent it.

(b) Erection of fences

8–04   The erection of a fence is one of the improvements that a tenant for life for the purposes of the Settled Land Act 1925 may carry out and have paid for from capital money without being called upon to repay by instalments. The scheme for improvements does not have to be submitted by the tenant for life for prior approval by the trustees or the court. The trustees are authorised to pay out the money on the certificate of the tenant for life's engineer or surveyor. The settled land may be mortgaged to raise money for this purpose.

3 Trusts of land

Trustees of land normally have all the powers of an absolute owner of property (Trusts of Land and Appointment of Trustees Act 1996, s.6(1)). This is subject to two qualifications. First, the powers must not be exercised in contravention of any other Act, rule of law or equity, or order including an order of the Charity Commissioners (s.6(6)–(8)). Secondly, a disposition creating a trust, such as a conveyance to more than one person, may validly restrict the trustees' powers (s.8).   **8–05**

4 Churchyards

The special legal rules that govern the property of the Church of England affect the fixing and fencing of the boundaries of churchyards. The care and maintenance of a churchyard is the responsibility of the parochial church council (Parochial Church Council (Powers) Measure 1956, s.4(ii)(c)), and that includes taking proceedings to settle boundary disputes where necessary (*St Edmundsbury and Ipswich Diocesan Board of Finance v Clark (No.2)* [1973] 1 W.L.R. 1572).   **8–06**

A faculty, granted by the chancellor of the diocese, is required for works in a churchyard, and this includes the erection of a boundary fence or wall. This applies both to consecrated and unconsecrated churchyards (Faculty Jurisdiction Measure 1964, s.7). A faculty will not be granted until it is established precisely where the boundary runs, so that the fence is erected in the right place (*Re St Peter and St Paul, Scrayingham* [1992] 1 W.L.R. 187). However, in one case a faculty was granted to keep a fence where it was accepted that "the present line of the fence represents a sensible demarcation line" (*Re St Clement's, Leigh-on-Sea* [1988] 1 W.L.R. 720, 726).

Appendix 1

Statutes

Law of Property Act 1925

s.38 Party structures

(1) Where under a disposition or other arrangement which, if a hold- **A1–01** ing in undivided shares had been permissible, would have created a tenancy in common, a wall or other structure is or is expressed to be made a party wall or structure, that structure shall be and remain severed vertically as between the respective owners, and the owner of each part shall have such rights to support and user over the rest of the structure as may be requisite for conferring rights corresponding to those which would have subsisted if a valid tenancy in common had been created.

(2) Any person interested may, in case of dispute, apply to the court for an order declaring the rights and interests under this section of the persons interested in any such party structure, and the court may make such order as it thinks fit.

Access to Neighbouring Land Act 1992

An Act to enable persons who desire to carry out works to any land which are reasonably necessary for the preservation of that land to obtain access to neighbouring land in order to do so; and for purposes connected therewith.

A1–02   **s.1 Access orders**

(1) A person—

    (a) who, for the purpose of carrying out works to any land (the "dominant land"), desires to enter upon any adjoining or adjacent land (the "servient land"); and

    (b) who needs, but does not have, the consent of some other person to that entry,

may make an application to the court for an order under this section ("an access order") against that other person.

(2) On an application under this section, the court shall make an access order if, and only if, it is satisfied—

    (a) that the works are reasonably necessary for the preservation of the whole or any part of the dominant land; and

    (b) that they cannot be carried out, or would be substantially more difficult to carry out, without entry upon the servient land;

but this subsection is subject to subsection (3) below.

(3) The court shall not make an access order in any case where it is satisfied that, were it to make such an order—

    (a) the respondent or any other person would suffer interference with, or disturbance of, his use or enjoyment of the servient land; or

    (b) the respondent, or any other person (whether of full age or capacity or not) in occupation of the whole or any part of the servient land, would suffer hardship;

to such a degree by reason of the entry (notwithstanding any requirement of this Act or any term or condition that may be imposed under it) that it would be unreasonable to make the order.

(4) Where the court is satisfied on an application under this section that it is reasonably necessary to carry out any basic preservation works to the dominant land, those works shall be taken for the purposes of this Act to be reasonably necessary for the preservation of the land; and in this subsection "basic preservation works" means any of the following, that is to say—

(a) the maintenance, repair or renewal of any part of a building or other structure comprised in, or situate on, the dominant land;

(b) the clearance, repair or renewal of any drain, sewer, pipe or cable so comprised or situate;

(c) the treatment, cutting back, felling, removal or replacement of any hedge, tree, shrub or other growing thing which is so comprised and which is, or is in danger of becoming, damaged, diseased, dangerous, insecurely rooted or dead;

(d) the filling in, or clearance, of any ditch so comprised;

but this subsection is without prejudice to the generality of the works which may, apart from it, be regarded by the court as reasonably necessary for the preservation of any land.

(5) If the court considers it fair and reasonable in all the circumstances of the case, works may be regarded for the purposes of this Act as being reasonably necessary for the preservation of any land (or, for the purposes of subsection (4) above, as being basic preservation works which it is reasonably necessary to carry out to any land) notwithstanding that the works incidentally involve—

(a) the making of some alteration, adjustment or improvement to the land, or

(b) the demolition of the whole or any part of a building or structure comprised in or situate upon the land.

(6) Where any works are reasonably necessary for the preservation of the whole or any part of the dominant land, the doing to the dominant land of anything which is requisite for, incidental to, or consequential on, the carrying out of those works shall be treated for the purposes of this Act as the carrying out of works which are reasonably necessary for the preservation of that land; and references in this Act to works, or to the carrying out of works, shall be construed accordingly.

(7) Without prejudice to the generality of subsection (6) above, if it is reasonably necessary for a person to inspect the dominant land—

(a) for the purpose of ascertaining whether any works may be reasonably necessary for the preservation of the whole or any part of that land;

(b) for the purpose of making any map or plan, or ascertaining the course of any drain, sewer, pipe or cable, in preparation for, or otherwise in connection with, the carrying out of works which are so reasonably necessary; or

(c) otherwise in connection with the carrying out of any such works;

the making of such an inspection shall be taken for the purposes of this Act to be the carrying out to the dominant land of works which are reasonably necessary for the preservation of that land; and references in this Act to works, or to the carrying out of works, shall be construed accordingly.

A1–03 **s.2 Terms and conditions of access orders**

(1) An access order shall specify—

(a) the works to the dominant land that may be carried out by entering upon the servient land in pursuance of the order;

(b) the particular area of servient land that may be entered upon by virtue of the order for the purpose of carrying out those works to the dominant land; and

(c) the date on which, or the period during which, the land may be so entered upon;

and in the following provisions of this Act any reference to the servient land is a reference to the area specified in the order in pursuance of paragraph (b) above.

(2) An access order may impose upon the applicant or the respondent such terms and conditions as appear to the court to be reasonably necessary for the purpose of avoiding or restricting—

(a) any loss, damage, or injury which might otherwise be caused to the respondent or any other person by reason of the entry authorised by the order; or

(b) any inconvenience or loss of privacy that might otherwise be so caused to the respondent or any other person.

(3) Without prejudice to the generality of subsection (2) above, the terms and conditions which may be imposed under that subsection include provisions with respect to—

(a) the manner in which the specified works are to be carried out;

(b) the days on which, and the hours between which, the work involved may be executed;

(c) the persons who may undertake the carrying out of the specified works or enter upon the servient land under or by virtue of the order;

(d) the taking of any such precautions by the applicant as may be specified in the order.

(4) An access order may also impose terms and conditions—

(a) requiring the applicant to pay, or to secure that such person connected with him as may be specified in the order pays, compensation for—

(i) any loss, damage or injury, or
(ii) any substantial loss of privacy or other substantial inconvenience,

which will, or might, be caused to the respondent or any other person by reason of the entry authorised by the order;

(b) requiring the applicant to secure that he, or such person connected with him as may be specified in the order, is insured against any such risks as may be so specified; or

(c) requiring such a record to be made of the condition of the servient land, or of such part of it as may be so specified, as the court may consider expedient with a view to facilitating the determination of any question that may arise concerning damage to that land.

(5) An access order may include provision requiring the applicant to pay the respondent such sum by way of consideration for the privilege of entering the servient land in pursuance of the order as appears to the court to be fair and reasonable having regard to all the circumstances of the case, including, in particular—

(a) the likely financial advantage of the order to the applicant and any persons connected with him; and

(b) the degree of inconvenience likely to be caused to the respondent or any other person by the entry;

but no payment shall be ordered under this subsection if and to the extent that the works which the applicant desires to carry out by means of the entry are works to residential land.

(6) For the purposes of subsection (5)(a) above, the likely financial advantage of an access order to the applicant and any persons connected with him shall in all cases be taken to be a sum of money equal to the greater of the following amounts, that is to say—

(a) the amount (if any) by which so much of any likely increase in the value of any land—

(i) which consists of or includes the dominant land; and
(ii) which is owned or occupied by the same person as the dominant land;

as may reasonably be regarded as attributable to the carrying out of the specified works exceeds the likely cost of carrying out those works with the benefit of the access order; and

(b) the difference (if it would have been possible to carry out the specified works without entering upon the servient land) between—

(i) the likely cost of carrying out those works without entering upon the servient land; and
(ii) the likely cost of carrying them out with the benefit of the access order.

(7) For the purposes of subsection (5) above, "residential land" means so much of any land as consists of—

(a) a dwelling or part of a dwelling;

(b) a garden, yard, private garage or outbuilding which is used and enjoyed wholly or mainly with a dwelling; or

(c) in the case of a building which includes one or more dwellings, any part of the building which is used and enjoyed wholly or mainly with those dwellings or any of them.

(8) The persons who are to be regarded for the purposes of this section as "connected with" the applicant are—

(a) the owner of any estate or interest in, or right over, the whole or any part of the dominant land;

(b) the occupier of the whole or any part of the dominant land; and

(c) any person whom the applicant may authorise under section 3(7) below to exercise the power of entry conferred by the access order.

(9) The court may make provision—

(a) for the reimbursement by the applicant of any expenses reasonably incurred by the respondent in connection with the application which are not otherwise recoverable as costs;

(b) for the giving of security by the applicant for any sum that might become payable to the respondent or any other person by virtue of this section or section 3 below.

s.3 Effect of access order

A1–04

(1) An access order requires the respondent, so far as he has power to do so, to permit the applicant or any of his associates to do anything which the applicant or associate is authorised or required to do under or by virtue of the order or this section.

(2) Except as otherwise provided by or under this Act, an access order authorises the applicant or any of his associates, without the consent of the respondent—

(a) to enter upon the servient land for the purpose of carrying out the specified works;

(b) to bring on to that land, leave there during the period permitted by the order and, before the end of that period, remove, such materials, plant and equipment as are reasonably necessary for the carrying out of those works; and

(c) to bring on to that land any waste arising from the carrying out of those works, if it is reasonably necessary to do so in the course of removing it from the dominant land;

but nothing in this Act or in any access order shall authorise the applicant or any of his associates to leave anything in, on or over the servient land (otherwise than in discharge of their duty to make good that land) after their entry for the purpose of carrying out works to the dominant land ceases to be authorised under or by virtue of the order.

(3) An access order requires the applicant—

(a) to secure that any waste arising from the carrying out of the specified works is removed from the servient land forthwith;

(b) to secure that, before the entry ceases to be authorised under or by virtue of the order, the servient land is, so far as reasonably practicable, made good; and

(c) to indemnify the respondent against any damage which may be caused to the servient land or any goods by the applicant or any of his associates which would not have been so caused had the order not been made;

but this subsection is subject to subsections (4) and (5) below.

(4) In making an access order, the court may vary or exclude, in whole or in part—

(a) any authorisation that would otherwise be conferred by subsection (2)(b) or (c) above; or

(b) any requirement that would otherwise be imposed by subsection (3) above.

(5) Without prejudice to the generality of subsection (4) above, if the court is satisfied that it is reasonably necessary for any such waste as may arise from the carrying out of the specified works to be left on the servient land for some period before removal, the access order may, in place of subsection (3)(a) above, include provision—

(a) authorising the waste to be left on that land for such period as may be permitted by the order; and

(b) requiring the applicant to secure that the waste is removed before the end of that period.

(6) Where the applicant or any of his associates is authorised or required under or by virtue of an access order or this section to enter, or do any other thing, upon the servient land, he shall not (as respects that access order) be taken to be a trespasser from the beginning on account of his, or any other person's, subsequent conduct.

(7) For the purposes of this section, the applicant's "associates" are such number of persons (whether or not servants or agents of his) whom he may reasonably authorise under this subsection to exercise the power of entry conferred by the access order as may be reasonably necessary for carrying out the specified works.

s.4 Persons bound by access order, unidentified persons and bar on contracting out

(1) In addition to the respondent, an access order shall, subject to the provisions of the Land Charges Act 1972 and the Land Registration Act 2002, be binding on—

(a) any of his successors in title to the servient land; and

(b) any person who has an estate or interest in, or right over, the whole or any part of the servient land which was created after the making of the order and who derives his title to that estate, interest or right under the respondent;

and references to the respondent shall be construed accordingly.

(2) If and to the extent that the court considers it just and equitable to allow him to do so, a person on whom an access order becomes binding by virtue of subsection (1)(a) or (b) above shall be entitled, as respects anything falling to be done after the order becomes binding on him, to enforce the order or any of its terms or conditions as if he were the respondent, and references to the respondent shall be construed accordingly.

(3) Rules of court may—

(a) provide a procedure which may be followed where the applicant does not know, and cannot reasonably ascertain, the name of any person whom he desires to make respondent to the application; and

(b) make provision enabling such an applicant to make such a person respondent by description instead of by name;

and in this subsection "applicant" includes a person who proposes to make an application for an access order.

(4) Any agreement, whenever made, shall be void if and to the extent that it would, apart from this subsection, prevent a person from applying for an access order or restrict his right to do so.

s.5 Registration of access orders and of applications for such orders

(1) In section 6(1) of the Land Charges Act 1972 (which specifies the writs and orders affecting land that may be entered in the register) after paragraph (c) there shall be added—

"(d) any access order under the Access to Neighbouring Land Act 1992."

(2) [. . .]

(3) [. . .]

(4) In any case where—

(a) an access order is discharged under section 6(1)(a) below; and

(b) the order has been protected by an entry registered under the Land Charges Act 1972 or by a notice or caution under the Land Registration Act 2002;

the court may by order direct that the entry, notice or caution shall be cancelled.

(5) The rights conferred on a person by or under an access order are not capable of constituting an overriding interest within paragraph 2 of Schedule 1 or 3 to the Land Registration Act 2002 (overriding status of interest of person in actual occupation).

(6) An application for an access order shall be regarded as a pending land action for the purposes of the Land Charges Act 1972 and the Land Registration Act 2002.

A1–07   **s.6 Variation of orders and damages for breach**

(1) Where an access order or an order under this subsection has been made, the court may, on the application of any party to the proceedings in which the order was made or of any other person on whom the order is binding—

(a) discharge or vary the order or any of its terms or conditions;

(b) suspend any of its terms or conditions; or

(c) revive any term or condition suspended under paragraph (b) above;

and in the application of subsections (1) and (2) of section 4 above in relation to an access order, any order under this subsection which relates to the access order shall be treated for the purposes of those subsections as included in the access order.

(2) If any person contravenes or fails to comply with any requirement, term or condition imposed upon him by or under this Act, the court may, without prejudice to any other remedy available, make an order for the payment of damages by him to any other person affected by the contravention or failure who makes an application for relief under this subsection.

s.7 Jurisdiction over, and allocation of, proceedings   A1–08

(1) The High Court and the county courts shall both have jurisdiction under this Act.

(2) In article 4 of the High Court and County Courts Jurisdiction Order 1991 (which provides that proceedings in which the county courts and the High Court both have jurisdiction may, subject to articles 5 and 6, be commenced either in a county court or in the High Court) for the words "and 6" there shall be substituted the words ", 6 and 6A" and after article 6 of that Order there shall be inserted—

"6A. Applications under section 1 of the Access to Neighbouring Land Act 1992 shall be commenced in a county court."

(3) The amendment by subsection (2) above of provisions contained in an order shall not be taken to have prejudiced any power to make further orders revoking or amending those provisions.
Interpretation and application.

s.8 Interpretation and application   A1–09

(1) Any reference in this Act to an "entry" upon any servient land includes a reference to the doing on that land of anything necessary for carrying out the works to the dominant land which are reasonably necessary for its preservation; and "enter" shall be construed accordingly.

(2) This Act applies in relation to any obstruction of, or other interference with, a right over, or interest in, any land as it applies in relation to an entry upon that land; and "enter" and "entry" shall be construed accordingly.

(3) In this Act—

"access order" has the meaning given by section 1(1) above;

"applicant" means a person making an application for an access order and, subject to section 4 above, "the respondent" means the respondent, or any of the respondents, to such an application;

"the court" means the High Court or a county court;

"the dominant land" and "the servient land" respectively have the meanings given by section 1(1) above, but subject, in the case of servient land, to section 2(1) above;

"land" does not include a highway;

"the specified works" means the works specified in the access order in pursuance of section 2(1)(a) above.

A1–10   s.9 Short title, commencement and extent

(1) This Act may be cited as the Access to Neighbouring Land Act 1992.

(2) This Act shall come into force on such day as the Lord Chancellor may by order made by statutory instrument appoint.

(3) This Act extends to England and Wales only.

Party Wall etc. Act 1996

An Act to make provision in respect of party walls, and excavation and construction in proximity to certain buildings or structures; and for connected purposes.

s.1 New building on line of junction

A1–11

(1) This section shall have effect where lands of different owners adjoin and—

(a) are not built on at the line of junction; or

(b) are built on at the line of junction only to the extent of a boundary wall (not being a party fence wall or the external wall of a building);

and either owner is about to build on any part of the line of junction.

(2) If a building owner desires to build a party wall or party fence wall on the line of junction he shall, at least one month before he intends the building work to start, serve on any adjoining owner a notice which indicates his desire to build and describes the intended wall.

(3) If, having been served with notice described in subsection (2), an adjoining owner serves on the building owner a notice indicating his consent to the building of a party wall or party fence wall—

(a) the wall shall be built half on the land of each of the two owners or in such other position as may be agreed between the two owners; and

(b) the expense of building the wall shall be from time to time defrayed by the two owners in such proportion as has regard to the use made or to be made of the wall by each of them and to the cost of labour and materials prevailing at the time when that use is made by each owner respectively.

(4) If, having been served with notice described in subsection (2), an adjoining owner does not consent under this subsection to the building of a party wall or party fence wall, the building owner may only build the wall—

(a) at his own expense; and

(b) as an external wall or a fence wall, as the case may be, placed wholly on his own land;

and consent under this subsection is consent by a notice served within the period of fourteen days beginning with the day on which the notice described in subsection (2) is served.

(5) If the building owner desires to build on the line of junction a wall placed wholly on his own land he shall, at least one month before he intends the building work to start, serve on any adjoining owner a notice which indicates his desire to build and describes the intended wall.

(6) Where the building owner builds a wall wholly on his own land in accordance with subsection (4) or (5) he shall have the right, at any time in the period which—

(a) begins one month after the day on which the notice mentioned in the subsection concerned was served, and

(b) ends twelve months after that day;

to place below the level of the land of the adjoining owner such projecting footings and foundations as are necessary for the construction of the wall.

(7) Where the building owner builds a wall wholly on his own land in accordance with subsection (4) or (5) he shall do so at his own expense and shall compensate any adjoining owner and any adjoining occupier for any damage to his property occasioned by—

(a) the building of the wall;

(b) the placing of any footings or foundations placed in accordance with subsection (6).

(8) Where any dispute arises under this section between the building owner and any adjoining owner or occupier it is to be determined in accordance with section 10.

A1–12   s.2 Repair etc. of party wall: rights of owner

(1) This section applies where lands of different owners adjoin and at the line of junction the said lands are built on or a boundary wall, being a party fence wall or the external wall of a building, has been erected.

(2) A building owner shall have the following rights—

(a) to underpin, thicken or raise a party structure, a party fence wall, or an external wall which belongs to the building owner and is built against a party structure or party fence wall;

(b) to make good, repair, or demolish and rebuild, a party structure or party fence wall in a case where such work is necessary on account of defect or want of repair of the structure or wall;

(c) to demolish a partition which separates buildings belonging to different owners but does not conform with statutory requirements and to build instead a party wall which does so conform;

(d) in the case of buildings connected by arches or structures over public ways or over passages belonging to other persons, to demolish the whole or part of such buildings, arches or structures which do not conform with statutory requirements and to rebuild them so that they do so conform;

(e) to demolish a party structure which is of insufficient strength or height for the purposes of any intended building of the building owner and to rebuild it of sufficient strength or height for the said purposes (including rebuilding to a lesser height or thickness where the rebuilt structure is of sufficient strength and height for the purposes of any adjoining owner);

(f) to cut into a party structure for any purpose (which may be or include the purpose of inserting a damp proof course);

(g) to cut away from a party wall, party fence wall, external wall or boundary wall any footing or any projecting chimney breast, jamb or flue, or other projection on or over the land of the building owner in order to erect, raise or underpin any such wall or for any other purpose;

(h) to cut away or demolish parts of any wall or building of an adjoining owner overhanging the land of the building owner or overhanging a party wall, to the extent that it is necessary to cut away or demolish the parts to enable a vertical wall to be erected or raised against the wall or building of the adjoining owner;

(j) to cut into the wall of an adjoining owner's building in order to insert a flashing or other weather-proofing of a wall erected against that wall;

(k) to execute any other necessary works incidental to the connection of a party structure with the premises adjoining it;

(l) to raise a party fence wall, or to raise such a wall for use as a party wall, and to demolish a party fence wall and rebuild it as a party fence wall or as a party wall;

(m) subject to the provisions of section 11(7), to reduce, or to demolish and rebuild, a party wall or party fence wall to—

(i) a height of not less than two metres where the wall is not used by an adjoining owner to any greater extent than a boundary wall; or

(ii) a height currently enclosed upon by the building of an adjoining owner;

(n) to expose a party wall or party structure hitherto enclosed subject to providing adequate weathering.

(3) Where work mentioned in paragraph (a) of subsection (2) is not necessary on account of defect or want of repair of the structure or wall concerned, the right falling within that paragraph is exercisable—

(a) subject to making good all damage occasioned by the work to the adjoining premises or to their internal furnishings and decorations; and

(b) where the work is to a party structure or external wall, subject to carrying any relevant flues and chimney stacks up to such a height and in such materials as may be agreed between the building owner and the adjoining owner concerned or, in the event of dispute, determined in accordance with section 10;

and relevant flues and chimney stacks are those which belong to an adjoining owner and either form part of or rest on or against the party structure or external wall.

(4) The right falling within subsection (2)(e) is exercisable subject to—

(a) making good all damage occasioned by the work to the adjoining premises or to their internal furnishings and decorations; and

(b) carrying any relevant flues and chimney stacks up to such a height and in such materials as may be agreed between the building owner and the adjoining owner concerned or, in the event of dispute, determined in accordance with section 10;

and relevant flues and chimney stacks are those which belong to an adjoining owner and either form part of or rest on or against the party structure.

(5) Any right falling within subsection (2)(f), (g) or (h) is exercisable subject to making good all damage occasioned by the work to the adjoining premises or to their internal furnishings and decorations.

(6) The right falling within subsection (2)(j) is exercisable subject to making good all damage occasioned by the work to the wall of the adjoining owner's building.

(7) The right falling within subsection (2)(m) is exercisable subject to—

(a) reconstructing any parapet or replacing an existing parapet with another one; or

(b) constructing a parapet where one is needed but did not exist before.

(8) For the purposes of this section a building or structure which was erected before the day on which this Act was passed shall be deemed to conform with statutory requirements if it conforms with the statutes regulating buildings or structures on the date on which it was erected.

s.3 Party structure notices   A1–13

(1) Before exercising any right conferred on him by section 2 a building owner shall serve on any adjoining owner a notice (in this Act referred to as a "party structure notice") stating—

(a) the name and address of the building owner;

(b) the nature and particulars of the proposed work including, in cases where the building owner proposes to construct special foundations, plans, sections and details of construction of the special foundations together with reasonable particulars of the loads to be carried thereby; and

(c) the date on which the proposed work will begin.

(2) A party structure notice shall—

(a) be served at least two months before the date on which the proposed work will begin;

(b) cease to have effect if the work to which it relates—

    (i) has not begun within the period of twelve months beginning with the day on which the notice is served; and

    (ii) is not prosecuted with due diligence.

(3) Nothing in this section shall—

(a) prevent a building owner from exercising with the consent in writing of the adjoining owners and of the adjoining occupiers any right conferred on him by section 2; or

(b) require a building owner to serve any party structure notice before complying with any notice served under any statutory provisions relating to dangerous or neglected structures.

A1–14   **s.4 Counter notices**

(1) An adjoining owner may, having been served with a party structure notice serve on the building owner a notice (in this Act referred to as a "counter notice") setting out—

(a) in respect of a party fence wall or party structure, a requirement that the building owner build in or on the wall or structure to which the notice relates such chimney copings, breasts, jambs or flues, or such piers or recesses or other like works, as may reasonably be required for the convenience of the adjoining owner;

(b) in respect of special foundations to which the adjoining owner consents under section 7(4) below, a requirement that the special foundations—

    (i) be placed at a specified greater depth than that proposed by the building owner; or

    (ii) be constructed of sufficient strength to bear the load to be carried by columns of any intended building of the adjoining owner,

or both.

(2) A counter notice shall—

(a) specify the works required by the notice to be executed and shall be accompanied by plans, sections and particulars of such works; and

(b) be served within the period of one month beginning with the day on which the party structure notice is served.

(3) A building owner on whom a counter notice has been served shall comply with the requirements of the counter notice unless the execution of the works required by the counter notice would—

(a) be injurious to him;

(b) cause unnecessary inconvenience to him; or

(c) cause unnecessary delay in the execution of the works pursuant to the party structure notice.

s.5 Disputes arising under sections 3 and 4   A1–15

If an owner on whom a party structure notice or a counter notice has been served does not serve a notice indicating his consent to it within the period of fourteen days beginning with the day on which the party structure notice or counter notice was served, he shall be deemed to have dissented from the notice and a dispute shall be deemed to have arisen between the parties.

s.6 Adjacent excavation and construction   A1–16

(1) This section applies where—

(a) a building owner proposes to excavate, or excavate for and erect a building or structure, within a distance of three metres measured horizontally from any part of a building or structure of an adjoining owner; and

(b) any part of the proposed excavation, building or structure will within those three metres extend to a lower level than the level of the bottom of the foundations of the building or structure of the adjoining owner.

(2) This section also applies where—

(a) a building owner proposes to excavate, or excavate for and erect a building or structure, within a distance of six metres measured horizontally from any part of a building or structure of an adjoining owner; and

(b) any part of the proposed excavation, building or structure will within those six metres meet a plane drawn downwards in the direction of the excavation, building or structure of the building owner at an angle of forty-five degrees to the horizontal from the line formed by the intersection of the plane of the level of the bottom of the foundations of the building or structure of the adjoining owner with the plane of the external face of the external wall of the building or structure of the adjoining owner.

(3) The building owner may, and if required by the adjoining owner shall, at his own expense underpin or otherwise strengthen or safeguard the foundations of the building or structure of the adjoining owner so far as may be necessary.

(4) Where the buildings or structures of different owners are within the respective distances mentioned in subsections (1) and (2) the owners of those buildings or structures shall be deemed to be adjoining owners for the purposes of this section.

(5) In any case where this section applies the building owner shall, at least one month before beginning to excavate, or excavate for and erect a building or structure, serve on the adjoining owner a notice indicating his proposals and stating whether he proposes to underpin or otherwise strengthen or safeguard the foundations of the building or structure of the adjoining owner.

(6) The notice referred to in subsection (5) shall be accompanied by plans and sections showing—

(a) the site and depth of any excavation the building owner proposes to make;

(b) if he proposes to erect a building or structure, its site.

(7) If an owner on whom a notice referred to in subsection (5) has been served does not serve a notice indicating his consent to it within the period of fourteen days beginning with the day on which the notice referred to in subsection (5) was served, he shall be deemed to have dissented from the notice and a dispute shall be deemed to have arisen between the parties.

(8) The notice referred to in subsection (5) shall cease to have effect if the work to which the notice relates—

(a) has not begun within the period of twelve months beginning with the day on which the notice was served; and

(b) is not prosecuted with due diligence.

(9) On completion of any work executed in pursuance of this section the building owner shall if so requested by the adjoining owner supply him with particulars including plans and sections of the work.

(10) Nothing in this section shall relieve the building owner from any liability to which he would otherwise be subject for injury to any adjoining owner or any adjoining occupier by reason of work executed by him.

s.7 Compensation etc.

A1–17

(1) A building owner shall not exercise any right conferred on him by this Act in such a manner or at such time as to cause unnecessary inconvenience to any adjoining owner or to any adjoining occupier.

(2) The building owner shall compensate any adjoining owner and any adjoining occupier for any loss or damage which may result to any of them by reason of any work executed in pursuance of this Act.

(3) Where a building owner in exercising any right conferred on him by this Act lays open any part of the adjoining land or building he shall at his own expense make and maintain so long as may be necessary a proper hoarding, shoring or fans or temporary construction for the protection of the adjoining land or building and the security of any adjoining occupier.

(4) Nothing in this Act shall authorise the building owner to place special foundations on land of an adjoining owner without his previous consent in writing.

(5) Any works executed in pursuance of this Act shall—

(a) comply with the provisions of statutory requirements; and

(b) be executed in accordance with such plans, sections and particulars as may be agreed between the owners or in the event of dispute determined in accordance with section 10;

and no deviation shall be made from those plans, sections and particulars except such as may be agreed between the owners (or surveyors acting on their behalf) or in the event of dispute determined in accordance with section 10.

A1–18   **s.8 Rights of entry**

(1) A building owner, his servants, agents and workmen may during usual working hours enter and remain on any land or premises for the purpose of executing any work in pursuance of this Act and may remove any furniture or fittings or take any other action necessary for that purpose.

(2) If the premises are closed, the building owner, his agents and workmen may, if accompanied by a constable or other police officer, break open any fences or doors in order to enter the premises.

(3) No land or premises may be entered by any person under subsection (1) unless the building owner serves on the owner and the occupier of the land or premises—

  (a) in case of emergency, such notice of the intention to enter as may be reasonably practicable;

  (b) in any other case, such notice of the intention to enter as complies with subsection (4).

(4) Notice complies with this subsection if it is served in a period of not less than fourteen days ending with the day of the proposed entry.

(5) A surveyor appointed or selected under section 10 may during usual working hours enter and remain on any land or premises for the purpose of carrying out the object for which he is appointed or selected.

(6) No land or premises may be entered by a surveyor under subsection (5) unless the building owner who is a party to the dispute concerned serves on the owner and the occupier of the land or premises—

  (a) in case of emergency, such notice of the intention to enter as may be reasonably practicable;

  (b) in any other case, such notice of the intention to enter as complies with subsection (4).

s.9 Easements

Nothing in this Act shall—

    (a) authorise any interference with an easement of light or other easements in or relating to a party wall; or

    (b) prejudicially affect any right of any person to preserve or restore any right or other thing in or connected with a party wall in case of the party wall being pulled down or rebuilt.

s.10 Resolution of disputes

(1) Where a dispute arises or is deemed to have arisen between a building owner and an adjoining owner in respect of any matter connected with any work to which this Act relates either—

    (a) both parties shall concur in the appointment of one surveyor (in this section referred to as an "agreed surveyor"); or

    (b) each party shall appoint a surveyor and the two surveyors so appointed shall forthwith select a third surveyor (all of whom are in this section referred to as "the three surveyors").

(2) All appointments and selections made under this section shall be in writing and shall not be rescinded by either party.

(3) If an agreed surveyor—

    (a) refuses to act;

    (b) neglects to act for a period of ten days beginning with the day on which either party serves a request on him;

    (c) dies before the dispute is settled; or

    (d) becomes or deems himself incapable of acting,

the proceedings for settling such dispute shall begin *de novo*.

(4) If either party to the dispute—

    (a) refuses to appoint a surveyor under subsection (1)(b); or

    (b) neglects to appoint a surveyor under subsection (1)(b) for a period of ten days beginning with the day on which the other party serves a request on him;

the other party may make the appointment on his behalf.

(5) If, before the dispute is settled, a surveyor appointed under paragraph (b) of subsection (1) by a party to the dispute dies, or becomes or deems himself incapable of acting, the party who appointed him may appoint another surveyor in his place with the same power and authority.

(6) If a surveyor—

    (a) appointed under paragraph (b) of subsection (1) by a party to the dispute; or

    (b) appointed under subsection (4) or (5);

refuses to act effectively, the surveyor of the other party may proceed to act ex parte and anything so done by him shall be as effectual as if he had been an agreed surveyor.

(7) If a surveyor—

    (a) appointed under paragraph (b) of subsection (1) by a party to the dispute; or

    (b) appointed under subsection (4) or (5);

neglects to act effectively for a period of ten days beginning with the day on which either party or the surveyor of the other party serves a request on him, the surveyor of the other party may proceed to act ex parte in respect of the subject matter of the request and anything so done by him shall be as effectual as if he had been an agreed surveyor.

(8) If either surveyor appointed under subsections (1)(b) by a party to the dispute refuses to select a third surveyor under subsections (1) or (9), or neglects to do so for a period of ten days beginning with the day on which the other surveyor serves a request on him—

    (a) the appointing officer; or

    (b) in cases where the relevant appointing officer or his employer is a party to the dispute, the Secretary of State;

may on the application of either surveyor select a third surveyor who shall have the same power and authority as if he had been selected under subsection (1) or subsection (9).

(9) If a third surveyor selected under subsection (1)(b)—

    (a) refuses to act;

    (b) neglects to act for a period of ten days beginning with the day on which either party or the surveyor appointed by either party serves a request on him; or

    (c) dies, or becomes or deems himself incapable of acting, before the dispute is settled;

the other two of the three surveyors shall forthwith select another surveyor in his place with the same power and authority.

(10) The agreed surveyor or as the case may be the three surveyors or any two of them shall settle by award any matter—

    (a) which is connected with any work to which this Act relates; and

    (b) which is in dispute between the building owner and the adjoining owner.

(11) Either of the parties or either of the surveyors appointed by the parties may call upon the third surveyor selected in pursuance of this section to determine the disputed matters and he shall make the necessary award.

(12) An award may determine—

    (a) the right to execute any work;

    (b) the time and manner of executing any work; and

    (c) any other matter arising out of or incidental to the dispute including the costs of making the award;

but any period appointed by the award for executing any work shall not unless otherwise agreed between the building owner and the adjoining owner begin to run until after the expiration of the period prescribed by this Act for service of the notice in respect of which the dispute arises or is deemed to have arisen.

(13) The reasonable costs incurred in—

    (a) making or obtaining an award under this section;

    (b) reasonable inspections of work to which the award relates; and

    (c) any other matter arising out of the dispute,

shall be paid by such of the parties as the surveyor or surveyors making the award determine.

(14) Where the surveyors appointed by the parties make an award the surveyors shall serve it forthwith on the parties.

(15) Where an award is made by the third surveyor—

(a) he shall, after payment of the costs of the award, serve it forthwith on the parties or their appointed surveyors; and

(b) if it is served on their appointed surveyors, they shall serve it forthwith on the parties.

(16) The award shall be conclusive and shall not except as provided by this section be questioned in any court.

(17) Either of the parties to the dispute may, within the period of fourteen days beginning with the day on which an award made under this section is served on him, appeal to the county court against the award and the county court may—

(a) rescind the award or modify it in such manner as the court thinks fit; and

(b) make such order as to costs as the court thinks fit.

A1–21   s.11 Expenses

(1) Except as provided under this section expenses of work under this Act shall be defrayed by the building owner.

(2) Any dispute as to responsibility for expenses shall be settled as provided in section 10.

(3) An expense mentioned in section 1(3)(b) shall be defrayed as there mentioned.

(4) Where work is carried out in exercise of the right mentioned in section 2(2)(a), and the work is necessary on account of defect or want of repair of the structure or wall concerned, the expenses shall be defrayed by the building owner and the adjoining owner in such proportion as has regard to—

(a) the use which the owners respectively make or may make of the structure or wall concerned; and

(b) responsibility for the defect or want of repair concerned, if more than one owner makes use of the structure or wall concerned.

(5) Where work is carried out in exercise of the right mentioned in section 2(2)(b) the expenses shall be defrayed by the building owner and the adjoining owner in such proportion as has regard to—

(a) the use which the owners respectively make or may make of the structure or wall concerned; and

(b) responsibility for the defect or want of repair concerned, if more than one owner makes use of the structure or wall concerned.

(6) Where the adjoining premises are laid open in exercise of the right mentioned in section 2(2)(e) a fair allowance in respect of disturbance and inconvenience shall be paid by the building owner to the adjoining owner or occupier.

(7) Where a building owner proposes to reduce the height of a party wall or party fence wall under section 2(2)(m) the adjoining owner may serve a counter notice under section 4 requiring the building owner to maintain the existing height of the wall, and in such case the adjoining owner shall pay to the building owner a due proportion of the cost of the wall so far as it exceeds—

(a) two metres in height; or

(b) the height currently enclosed upon by the building of the adjoining owner.

(8) Where the building owner is required to make good damage under this Act the adjoining owner has a right to require that the expenses of such making good be determined in accordance with section 10 and paid to him in lieu of the carrying out of work to make the damage good.

(9) Where—

(a) works are carried out; and

(b) some of the works are carried out at the request of the adjoining owner or in pursuance of a requirement made by him;

he shall defray the expenses of carrying out the works requested or required by him.

(10) Where—

    (a) consent in writing has been given to the construction of special foundations on land of an adjoining owner; and

    (b) the adjoining owner erects any building or structure and its cost is found to be increased by reason of the existence of the said foundations;

the owner of the building to which the said foundations belong shall, on receiving an account with any necessary invoices and other supporting documents within the period of two months beginning with the day of the completion of the work by the adjoining owner, repay to the adjoining owner so much of the cost as is due to the existence of the said foundations.

(11) Where use is subsequently made by the adjoining owner of work carried out solely at the expense of the building owner the adjoining owner shall pay a due proportion of the expenses incurred by the building owner in carrying out that work; and for this purpose he shall be taken to have incurred expenses calculated by reference to what the cost of the work would be if it were carried out at the time when that subsequent use is made.

A1–22   **s.12 Security for expenses**

(1) An adjoining owner may serve a notice requiring the building owner before he begins any work in the exercise of the rights conferred by this Act to give such security as may be agreed between the owners or in the event of dispute determined in accordance with section 10.

(2) Where—

    (a) in the exercise of the rights conferred by this Act an adjoining owner requires the building owner to carry out any work the expenses of which are to be defrayed in whole or in part by the adjoining owner; or

    (b) an adjoining owner serves a notice on the building owner under subsection (1);

the building owner may before beginning the work to which the requirement or notice relates serve a notice on the adjoining owner requiring him to give such security as may be agreed between the owners or in the event of dispute determined in accordance with section 10.

(3) If within the period of one month beginning with—

(a) the day on which a notice is served under subsection (2); or

(b) in the event of dispute, the date of the determination by the surveyor or surveyors;

the adjoining owner does not comply with the notice or the determination, the requirement or notice by him to which the building owner's notice under that subsection relates shall cease to have effect.

s.13 Account for work carried out   A1–23

(1) Within the period of two months beginning with the day of the completion of any work executed by a building owner of which the expenses are to be wholly or partially defrayed by an adjoining owner in accordance with section 11 the building owner shall serve on the adjoining owner an account in writing showing—

(a) particulars and expenses of the work; and

(b) any deductions to which the adjoining owner or any other person is entitled in respect of old materials or otherwise;

and in preparing the account the work shall be estimated and valued at fair average rates and prices according to the nature of the work, the locality and the cost of labour and materials prevailing at the time when the work is executed.

(2) Within the period of one month beginning with the day of service of the said account the adjoining owner may serve on the building owner a notice stating any objection he may have thereto and thereupon a dispute shall be deemed to have arisen between the parties.

(3) If within that period of one month the adjoining owner does not serve notice under subsection (2) he shall be deemed to have no objection to the account.

s.14 Settlement of account   A1–24

(1) All expenses to be defrayed by an adjoining owner in accordance with an account served under section 13 shall be paid by the adjoining owner.

(2) Until an adjoining owner pays to the building owner such expenses as aforesaid the property in any works executed under this Act to which the expenses relate shall be vested solely in the building owner.

A1–25   **s.15 Service of notices etc.**

(1) A notice or other document required or authorised to be served under this Act may be served on a person—

    (a) by delivering it to him in person;

    (b) by sending it by post to him at his usual or last-known residence or place of business in the United Kingdom; or

    (c) in the case of a body corporate, by delivering it to the secretary or clerk of the body corporate at its registered or principal office or sending it by post to the secretary or clerk of that body corporate at that office.

(2) In the case of a notice or other document required or authorised to be served under this Act on a person as owner of premises, it may alternatively be served by—

    (a) addressing it "the owner" of the premises (naming them); and

    (b) delivering it to a person on the premises or, if no person to whom it can be delivered is found there, fixing it to a conspicuous part of the premises.

A1–26   **s.16 Offences**

(1) If—

    (a) an occupier of land or premises refuses to permit a person to do anything which he is entitled to do with regard to the land or premises under section 8(1) or (5); and

    (b) the occupier knows or has reasonable cause to believe that the person is so entitled;

the occupier is guilty of an offence.

(2) If—

   (a) a person hinders or obstructs a person in attempting to do anything which he is entitled to do with regard to land or premises under section 8(1) or (5); and

   (b) the first-mentioned person knows or has reasonable cause to believe that the other person is so entitled;

the first-mentioned person is guilty of an offence.

(3) A person guilty of an offence under subsection (1) or (2) is liable on summary conviction to a fine of an amount not exceeding level 3 on the standard scale.

s.17 Recovery of sums

A1–27

Any sum payable in pursuance of this Act (otherwise than by way of fine) shall be recoverable summarily as a civil debt.

s.18 Exception in case of Temples etc.

A1–28

(1) This Act shall not apply to land which is situated in inner London and in which there is an interest belonging to—

   (a) the Honourable Society of the Inner Temple;

   (b) the Honourable Society of the Middle Temple;

   (c) the Honourable Society of Lincoln's Inn; or

   (d) the Honourable Society of Gray's Inn.

(2) The reference in subsection (1) to inner London is to Greater London other than the outer London boroughs.

s.19 The Crown

A1–29

(1) This Act shall apply to land in which there is—

   (a) an interest belonging to Her Majesty in right of the Crown;

   (b) an interest belonging to a government department; or

   (c) an interest held in trust for Her Majesty for the purposes of any such department.

(2) This Act shall apply to—

(a) land which is vested in, but not occupied by, Her Majesty in right of the Duchy of Lancaster;

(b) land which is vested in, but not occupied by, the possessor for the time being of the Duchy of Cornwall.

A1–30 s.20 Interpretation

In this Act, unless the context otherwise requires, the following expressions have the meanings hereby respectively assigned to them—

"adjoining owner" and "adjoining occupier" respectively mean any owner and any occupier of land, buildings, storeys or rooms adjoining those of the building owner and for the purposes only of section 6 within the distances specified in that section;

"appointing officer" means the person appointed under this Act by the local authority to make such appointments as are required under section 10(8);

"building owner" means an owner of land who is desirous of exercising rights under this Act;

"foundation", in relation to a wall, means the solid ground or artificially formed support resting on solid ground on which the wall rests;

"owner" includes—

(a) a person in receipt of, or entitled to receive, the whole or part of the rents or profits of land;

(b) a person in possession of land, otherwise than as a mortgagee or as a tenant from year to year or for a lesser term or as a tenant at will;

(c) a purchaser of an interest in land under a contract for purchase or under an agreement for a lease, otherwise than under an agreement for a tenancy from year to year or for a lesser term;

"party fence wall" means a wall (not being part of a building) which stands on lands of different owners and is used or constructed to be used for separating such adjoining lands, but does not include a wall constructed on the land of one owner the artificially formed support of which projects into the land of another owner;

"party structure" means a party wall and also a floor partition or other structure separating buildings or parts of buildings approached solely by separate staircases or separate entrances;

"party wall" means—

    (a) a wall which forms part of a building and stands on lands of different owners to a greater extent than the projection of any artificially formed support on which the wall rests; and

    (b) so much of a wall not being a wall referred to in paragraph (a) above as separates buildings belonging to different owners;

"special foundations" means foundations in which an assemblage of beams or rods is employed for the purpose of distributing any load; and

"surveyor" means any person not being a party to the matter appointed or selected under section 10 to determine disputes in accordance with the procedures set out in this Act.

Other statutory provisions

A1–31

(1) The Secretary of State may by order amend or repeal any provision of a private or local Act passed before or in the same session as this Act, if it appears to him necessary or expedient to do so in consequence of this Act.

(2) An order under subsection (1) may—

    (a) contain such savings or transitional provisions as the Secretary of State thinks fit;

    (b) make different provision for different purposes.

(3) The power to make an order under subsection (1) shall be exercisable by statutory instrument subject to annulment in pursuance of a resolution of either House of Parliament.

s.22 Short title, commencement and extent

A1–32

(1) This Act may be cited as the Party Wall etc. Act 1996.

(2) This Act shall come into force in accordance with provision made by the Secretary of State by order made by statutory instrument.

(3) An order under subsection (2) may—

    (a) contain such savings or transitional provisions as the Secretary of State thinks fit;

    (b) make different provision for different purposes.

(4) This Act extends to England and Wales only.

Land Registration Act 2002
Part 6 Registration: General Boundaries

A1–33   **s.60 Boundaries**

(1) The boundary of a registered estate as shown for the purposes of the register is a general boundary, unless shown as determined under this section.

(2) A general boundary does not determine the exact line of the boundary.

(3) Rules may make provision enabling or requiring the exact line of the boundary of a registered estate to be determined and may, in particular, make provision about—

    (a) the circumstances in which the exact line of a boundary may or must be determined;

    (b) how the exact line of a boundary may be determined;

    (c) procedure in relation to applications for determination; and

    (d) the recording of the fact of determination in the register or the index maintained under section 68.

(4) Rules under this section must provide for applications for determination to be made to the registrar.

A1–33.1   **s.61 Accretion and diluvion**

(1) The fact that a registered estate in land is shown in the register as having a particular boundary does not affect the operation of accretion or diluvion.

(2) An agreement about the operation of accretion or diluvion in relation to a registered estate in land has effect only if registered in accordance with rules.

Anti-social Behaviour Act 2003
Part 8 High Hedges

s.65 Complaints to which this Part applies

A1–34

(1) This Part applies to a complaint which—

   (a) is made for the purposes of this Part by an owner or occupier of a domestic property; and

   (b) alleges that his reasonable enjoyment of that property is being adversely affected by the height of a high hedge situated on land owned or occupied by another person.

(2) This Part also applies to a complaint which—

   (a) is made for the purposes of this Part by an owner of a domestic property that is for the time being unoccupied; and

   (b) alleges that the reasonable enjoyment of that property by a prospective occupier of that property would be adversely affected by the height of a high hedge situated on land owned or occupied by another person;

as it applies to a complaint falling within subsection (1).

(3) In relation to a complaint falling within subsection (2), references in sections 68 and 69 to the effect of the height of a high hedge on the complainant's reasonable enjoyment of a domestic property shall be read as references to the effect that it would have on the reasonable enjoyment of that property by a prospective occupier of the property.

(4) This Part does not apply to complaints about the effect of the roots of a high hedge.

(5) In this Part, in relation to a complaint –

   "complainant" means—

   (a) a person by whom the complaint is made; or

   (b) if every person who made the complaint ceases to be an owner or occupier of the domestic property specified in the complaint, any other person who is for the time being an owner or occupier of that property;

and references to the complainant include references to one or more of the complainants;

"the neighbouring land" means the land on which the high hedge is situated; and

"the relevant authority" means the local authority in whose area that land is situated.

A1–35   s.66 High hedges

(1) In this Part "high hedge" means so much of a barrier to light or access as—

   (a) is formed wholly or predominantly by a line of two or more evergreens; and

   (b) rises to a height of more than two metres above ground level.

(2) For the purposes of subsection (1) a line of evergreens is not to be regarded as forming a barrier to light or access if the existence of gaps significantly affects its overall effect as such a barrier at heights of more than two metres above ground level.

(3) In this section "evergreen" means an evergreen tree or shrub or a semi-evergreen tree or shrub.

A1–36   s.67 Domestic property

(1) In this Part "domestic property" means—

   (a) a dwelling; or

   (b) a garden or yard which is used and enjoyed wholly or mainly in connection with a dwelling.

(2) In subsection (1) "dwelling" means any building or part of a building occupied, or intended to be occupied, as a separate dwelling.

(3) A reference in this Part to a person's reasonable enjoyment of domestic property includes a reference to his reasonable enjoyment of a part of the property.

s.68 Procedure for dealing with complaints

(1) This section has effect where a complaint to which this Part applies—

- (a) is made to the relevant authority; and
- (b) is accompanied by such fee (if any) as the authority may determine.

(2) If the authority consider—

- (a) that the complainant has not taken all reasonable steps to resolve the matters complained of without proceeding by way of such a complaint to the authority; or
- (b) that the complaint is frivolous or vexatious;

the authority may decide that the complaint should not be proceeded with.

(3) If the authority do not so decide, they must decide—

- (a) whether the height of the high hedge specified in the complaint is adversely affecting the complainant's reasonable enjoyment of the domestic property so specified; and
- (b) if so, what action (if any) should be taken in relation to that hedge, in pursuance of a remedial notice under section 69, with a view to remedying the adverse effect or preventing its recurrence.

(4) If the authority decide under subsection (3) that action should be taken as mentioned in paragraph (b) of that subsection, they must as soon as is reasonably practicable—

- (a) issue a remedial notice under section 69 implementing their decision;
- (b) send a copy of that notice to the following persons, namely—
  - (i) every complainant; and
  - (ii) every owner and every occupier of the neighbouring land; and
- (c) notify each of those persons of the reasons for their decision.

(5) If the authority—

- (a) decide that the complaint should not be proceeded with; or
- (b) decide either or both of the issues specified in subsection (3) otherwise than in the complainant's favour;

they must as soon as is reasonably practicable notify the appropriate person or persons of any such decision and of their reasons for it.

(6) For the purposes of subsection (5)—

- (a) every complainant is an appropriate person in relation to a decision falling within paragraph (a) or (b) of that subsection; and
- (b) every owner and every occupier of the neighbouring land is an appropriate person in relation to a decision falling within paragraph (b) of that subsection.

(7) A fee determined under subsection (1)(b) must not exceed the amount prescribed in regulations made—

- (a) in relation to complaints relating to hedges situated in England, by the Secretary of State; and
- (b) in relation to complaints relating to hedges situated in Wales, by the National Assembly for Wales.

(8) A fee received by a local authority by virtue of subsection (1)(b) may be refunded by them in such circumstances and to such extent as they may determine.

A1–38   s.69 Remedial notices

(1) For the purposes of this Part a remedial notice is a notice—

- (a) issued by the relevant authority in respect of a complaint to which this Part applies; and
- (b) stating the matters mentioned in subsection (2).

(2) Those matters are—

- (a) that a complaint has been made to the authority under this Part about a high hedge specified in the notice which is situated on land so specified;

(b) that the authority have decided that the height of that hedge is adversely affecting the complainant's reasonable enjoyment of the domestic property specified in the notice;

(c) the initial action that must be taken in relation to that hedge before the end of the compliance period;

(d) any preventative action that they consider must be taken in relation to that hedge at times following the end of that period while the hedge remains on the land; and

(e) the consequences under sections 75 and 77 of a failure to comply with the notice.

(3) The action specified in a remedial notice is not to require or involve—

(a) a reduction in the height of the hedge to less than two metres above ground level; or

(b) the removal of the hedge.

(4) A remedial notice shall take effect on its operative date.

(5) "The operative date" of a remedial notice is such date (falling at least 28 days after that on which the notice is issued) as is specified in the notice as the date on which it is to take effect.

(6) "The compliance period" in the case of a remedial notice is such reasonable period as is specified in the notice for the purposes of subsection (2)(c) as the period within which the action so specified is to be taken; and that period shall begin with the operative date of the notice.

(7) Subsections (4) to (6) have effect in relation to a remedial notice subject to—

(a) the exercise of any power of the relevant authority under section 70; and

(b) the operation of sections 71 to 73 in relation to the notice.

(8) While a remedial notice has effect, the notice—

(a) shall be a local land charge; and

(b) shall be binding on every person who is for the time being an owner or occupier of the land specified in the notice as the land where the hedge in question is situated.

(9) In this Part—

"initial action" means remedial action or preventative action, or both;

"remedial action" means action to remedy the adverse effect of the height of the hedge on the complainant's reasonable enjoyment of the domestic property in respect of which the complaint was made; and

"preventative action" means action to prevent the recurrence of the adverse effect.

A1–39   s.70 Withdrawal or relaxation of requirements of remedial notices

(1) The relevant authority may—

    (a) withdraw a remedial notice issued by them; or

    (b) waive or relax a requirement of a remedial notice so issued.

(2) The powers conferred by this section are exercisable both before and after a remedial notice has taken effect.

(3) Where the relevant authority exercise the powers conferred by this section, they must give notice of what they have done to—

    (a) every complainant; and

    (b) every owner and every occupier of the neighbouring land.

(4) The withdrawal of a remedial notice does not affect the power of the relevant authority to issue a further remedial notice in respect of the same hedge.

A1–40   s.71 Appeals against remedial notices and other decisions of relevant authorities

(1) Where the relevant authority—

    (a) issue a remedial notice;

    (b) withdraw such a notice; or

    (c) waive or relax the requirements of such a notice;

each of the persons falling within subsection (2) may appeal to the appeal authority against the issue or withdrawal of the notice or (as the case may be) the waiver or relaxation of its requirements.

(2) Those persons are—

(a) every person who is a complainant in relation to the complaint by reference to which the notice was given; and

(b) every person who is an owner or occupier of the neighbouring land.

(3) Where the relevant authority decide either or both of the issues specified in section 68(3) otherwise than in the complainant's favour, the complainant may appeal to the appeal authority against the decision.

(4) An appeal under this section must be made before—

(a) the end of the period of 28 days beginning with the relevant date; or

(b) such later time as the appeal authority may allow.

(5) In subsection (4) "the relevant date"—

(a) in the case of an appeal against the issue of a remedial notice, means the date on which the notice was issued; and

(b) in the case of any other appeal under this section, means the date of the notification given by the relevant authority under section 68 or 70 of the decision in question.

(6) Where an appeal is duly made under subsection (1), the notice or (as the case may be) withdrawal, waiver or relaxation in question shall not have effect pending the final determination or withdrawal of the appeal.

(7) In this Part "the appeal authority" means—

(a) in relation to appeals relating to hedges situated in England, the Secretary of State; and

(b) in relation to appeals relating to hedges situated in Wales, the National Assembly for Wales.

A1–41   **s.72 Appeals procedure**

(1) The appeal authority may by regulations make provision with respect to—

  (a) the procedure which is to be followed in connection with appeals to that authority under section 71; and

  (b) other matters consequential on or connected with such appeals.

(2) Regulations under this section may, in particular, make provision—

  (a) specifying the grounds on which appeals may be made;

  (b) prescribing the manner in which appeals are to be made;

  (c) requiring persons making appeals to send copies of such documents as may be prescribed to such persons as may be prescribed;

  (d) requiring local authorities against whose decisions appeals are made to send to the appeal authority such documents as may be prescribed;

  (e) specifying, where a local authority are required by virtue of paragraph (d) to send the appeal authority a statement indicating the submissions which they propose to put forward on the appeal, the matters to be included in such a statement;

  (f) prescribing the period within which a requirement imposed by the regulations is to be complied with;

  (g) enabling such a period to be extended by the appeal authority;

  (h) for a decision on an appeal to be binding on persons falling within section 71(2) in addition to the person by whom the appeal was made;

  (i) for incidental or ancillary matters, including the awarding of costs.

(3) Where an appeal is made to the appeal authority under section 71 the appeal authority may appoint a person to hear and determine the appeal on its behalf.

(4) The appeal authority may require such a person to exercise on its behalf any functions which—

(a) are conferred on the appeal authority in connection with such an appeal by section 71 or 73 or by regulations under this section; and

(b) are specified in that person's appointment;

and references to the appeal authority in section 71 or 73 or in any regulations under this section shall be construed accordingly.

(5) The appeal authority may pay a person appointed under subsection (3) such remuneration as it may determine.

(6) Regulations under this section may provide for any provision of Schedule 20 to the Environment Act 1995 (c. 25) (delegation of appellate functions) to apply in relation to a person appointed under subsection (3) with such modifications (if any) as may be prescribed.

(7) In this section, "prescribed" means prescribed by regulations made by the appeal authority.

s.73 Determination or withdrawal of appeals

A1–42

(1) On an appeal under section 71 the appeal authority may allow or dismiss the appeal, either in whole or in part.

(2) Where the appeal authority decides to allow such an appeal to any extent, it may do such of the following as it considers appropriate—

(a) quash a remedial notice or decision to which the appeal relates;

(b) vary the requirements of such a notice; or

(c) in a case where no remedial notice has been issued, issue on behalf of the relevant authority a remedial notice that could have been issued by the relevant authority on the complaint in question.

(3) On an appeal under section 71 relating to a remedial notice, the appeal authority may also correct any defect, error or misdescription in the notice if it is satisfied that the correction will not cause injustice to any person falling within section 71(2).

(4) Once the appeal authority has made its decision on an appeal under section 71, it must, as soon as is reasonably practicable—

(a) give a notification of the decision; and

(b) if the decision is to issue a remedial notice or to vary or correct the requirements of such a notice, send copies of the notice as issued, varied or corrected;

to every person falling within section 71(2) and to the relevant authority.

(5) Where, in consequence of the appeal authority's decision on an appeal, a remedial notice is upheld or varied or corrected, the operative date of the notice shall be—

(a) the date of the appeal authority's decision; or

(b) such later date as may be specified in its decision.

(6) Where the person making an appeal under section 71 against a remedial notice withdraws his appeal, the operative date of the notice shall be the date on which the appeal is withdrawn.

(7) In any case falling within subsection (5) or (6), the compliance period for the notice shall accordingly run from the date which is its operative date by virtue of that subsection (and any period which may have started to run from a date preceding that on which the appeal was made shall accordingly be disregarded).

A1–43   s.74 Powers of entry for the purposes of complaints and appeals

(1) Where, under this Part, a complaint has been made or a remedial notice has been issued, a person authorised by the relevant authority may enter the neighbouring land in order to obtain information required by the relevant authority for the purpose of determining—

(a) whether this Part applies to the complaint;

(b) whether to issue or withdraw a remedial notice;

(c) whether to waive or relax a requirement of a remedial notice;

(d) whether a requirement of a remedial notice has been complied with.

(2) Where an appeal has been made under section 71, a person authorised—

(a) by the appeal authority; or

(b) by a person appointed to determine appeals on its behalf;

may enter the neighbouring land in order to obtain information required by the appeal authority, or by the person so appointed, for the purpose of determining an appeal under this Part.

(3) A person shall not enter land in the exercise of a power conferred by this section unless at least 24 hours' notice of the intended entry has been given to every occupier of the land.

(4) A person authorised under this section to enter land—

(a) shall, if so required, produce evidence of his authority before entering; and

(b) shall produce such evidence if required to do so at any time while he remains on the land.

(5) A person who enters land in the exercise of a power conferred by this section may—

(a) take with him such other persons as may be necessary;

(b) take with him equipment and materials needed in order to obtain the information required;

(c) take samples of any trees or shrubs that appear to him to form part of a high hedge.

(6) If, in the exercise of a power conferred by this section, a person enters land which is unoccupied or from which all of the persons occupying the land are temporarily absent, he must on his departure leave it as effectively secured against unauthorised entry as he found it.

(7) A person who intentionally obstructs a person acting in the exercise of the powers under this section is guilty of an offence and shall be liable, on summary conviction, to a fine not exceeding level 3 on the standard scale.

s.75 Offences

A1–44

(1) Where—

(a) a remedial notice requires the taking of any action; and

(b) that action is not taken in accordance with that notice within the compliance period or (as the case may be) by the subsequent time by which it is required to be taken;

every person who, at a relevant time, is an owner or occupier of the neighbouring land is guilty of an offence and shall be liable, on summary conviction, to a fine not exceeding level 3 on the standard scale.

(2) In subsection (1) "relevant time"—

(a) in relation to action required to be taken before the end of the compliance period, means a time after the end of that period and before the action is taken; and

(b) in relation to any preventative action which is required to be taken after the end of that period, means a time after that at which the action is required to be taken but before it is taken.

(3) In proceedings against a person for an offence under subsection (1) it shall be a defence for him to show that he did everything he could be expected to do to secure compliance with the notice.

(4) In any such proceedings against a person, it shall also be a defence for him to show, in a case in which he—

(a) is not a person to whom a copy of the remedial notice was sent in accordance with a provision of this Part; and

(b) is not assumed under subsection (5) to have had knowledge of the notice at the time of the alleged offence;

that he was not aware of the existence of the notice at that time.

(5) A person shall be assumed to have had knowledge of a remedial notice at any time if at that time—

(a) he was an owner of the neighbouring land; and

(b) the notice was at that time registered as a local land charge.

(6) Section 198 of the Law of Property Act 1925 (c.20) (constructive notice) shall be disregarded for the purposes of this section.

(7) Where a person is convicted of an offence under subsection (1) and it appears to the court—

(a) that a failure to comply with the remedial notice is continuing; and

(b) that it is within that person's power to secure compliance with the notice;

the court may, in addition to or instead of imposing a punishment, order him to take the steps specified in the order for securing compliance with the notice.

(8) An order under subsection (7) must require those steps to be taken within such reasonable period as may be fixed by the order.

(9) Where a person fails without reasonable excuse to comply with an order under subsection (7) he is guilty of an offence and shall be liable, on summary conviction, to a fine not exceeding level 3 on the standard scale.

(10) Where a person continues after conviction of an offence under subsection (9) (or of an offence under this subsection) to fail, without reasonable excuse, to take steps which he has been ordered to take under subsection (7), he is guilty of a further offence and shall be liable, on summary conviction, to a fine not exceeding one-twentieth of that level for each day on which the failure has so continued.

s.76 Power to require occupier to permit action to be taken by owner A1–45

Section 289 of the Public Health Act 1936 (c. 49) (power of court to require occupier to permit work to be done by owner) shall apply with any necessary modifications for the purpose of giving an owner of land to which a remedial notice relates the right, as against all other persons interested in the land, to comply with the notice.

s.77 Action by relevant authority A1–46

(1) This section applies where—

(a) a remedial notice requires the taking of any action; and

(b) that action is not taken in accordance with that notice within the compliance period or (as the case may be) after the end of that period when it is required to be taken by the notice.

(2) Where this section applies—

   (a) a person authorised by the relevant authority may enter the neighbouring land and take the required action; and

   (b) the relevant authority may recover any expenses reasonably incurred by that person in doing so from any person who is an owner or occupier of the land.

(3) Expenses recoverable under this section shall be a local land charge and binding on successive owners of the land and on successive occupiers of it.

(4) Where expenses are recoverable under this section from two or more persons, those persons shall be jointly and severally liable for the expenses.

(5) A person shall not enter land in the exercise of a power conferred by this section unless at least 7 days' notice of the intended entry has been given to every occupier of the land.

(6) A person authorised under this section to enter land—

   (a) shall, if so required, produce evidence of his authority before entering; and

   (b) shall produce such evidence if required to do so at any time while he remains on the land.

(7) A person who enters land in the exercise of a power conferred by this section may—

   (a) use a vehicle to enter the land;

   (b) take with him such other persons as may be necessary;

   (c) take with him equipment and materials needed for the purpose of taking the required action.

(8) If, in the exercise of a power conferred by this section, a person enters land which is unoccupied or from which all of the persons occupying the land are temporarily absent, he must on his departure leave it as effectively secured against unauthorised entry as he found it.

(9) A person who wilfully obstructs a person acting in the exercise of powers under this section to enter land and take action on that land is guilty of an offence and shall be liable, on summary conviction, to a fine not exceeding level 3 on the standard scale.

s.78 Offences committed by bodies corporate

(1) Where an offence under this Part committed by a body corporate is proved to have been committed with the consent or connivance of, or to be attributable to any neglect on the part of—

   (a) a director, manager, secretary or other similar officer of the body corporate; or

   (b) any person who was purporting to act in any such capacity;

he, as well as the body corporate, shall be guilty of that offence and be liable to be proceeded against and punished accordingly.

(2) Where the affairs of a body corporate are managed by its members, subsection (1) applies in relation to the acts and defaults of a member in connection with his functions of management as if he were a director of the body corporate.

s.79 Service of documents

(1) A notification or other document required to be given or sent to a person by virtue of this Part shall be taken to be duly given or sent to him if served in accordance with the following provisions of this section.

(2) Such a document may be served—

   (a) by delivering it to the person in question;

   (b) by leaving it at his proper address; or

   (c) by sending it by post to him at that address.

(3) Such a document may—

   (a) in the case of a body corporate, be served on the secretary or clerk of that body;

   (b) in the case of a partnership, be served on a partner or a person having the control or management of the partnership business.

(4) For the purposes of this section and of section 7 of the Interpretation Act 1978 (c.30) (service of documents by post) in its application to this section, a person's proper address shall be his last known address, except that—

(a) in the case of a body corporate or their secretary or clerk, it shall be the address of the registered or principal office of that body; and

(b) in the case of a partnership or person having the control or the management of the partnership business, it shall be the principal office of the partnership.

(5) For the purposes of subsection (4) the principal office of—

(a) a company registered outside the United Kingdom; or

(b) a partnership carrying on business outside the United Kingdom;

shall be their principal office within the United Kingdom.

(6) If a person has specified an address in the United Kingdom other than his proper address within the meaning of subsection (4) as the one at which he or someone on his behalf will accept documents of a particular description, that address shall also be treated for the purposes of this section and section 7 of the Interpretation Act 1978 as his proper address in connection with the service on him of a document of that description.

(7) Where—

(a) by virtue of this Part a document is required to be given or sent to a person who is an owner or occupier of any land; and

(b) the name or address of that person cannot be ascertained after reasonable inquiry;

the document may be served either by leaving it in the hands of a person who is or appears to be resident or employed on the land or by leaving it conspicuously affixed to some building or object on the land.

A1–49   **s.80 Documents in electronic form**

(1) A requirement of this Part—

(a) to send a copy of a remedial notice to a person; or

(b) to notify a person under section 68(4) of the reasons for the issue of a remedial notice;

is not capable of being satisfied by transmitting the copy or notification electronically or by making it available on a website.

(2) The delivery of any other document to a person (the "recipient") may be effected for the purposes of section 79(2)(a)—

(a) by transmitting it electronically; or

(b) by making it available on a website;

but only if it is transmitted or made available in accordance with subsections (3) or (5).

(3) A document is transmitted electronically in accordance with this subsection if—

(a) the recipient has agreed that documents may be delivered to him by being transmitted to an electronic address and in an electronic form specified by him for that purpose; and

(b) the document is a document to which that agreement applies and is transmitted to that address in that form.

(4) A document which is transmitted in accordance with subsection (3) by means of an electronic communications network shall, unless the contrary is proved, be treated as having been delivered at 9 a.m. on the working day immediately following the day on which it is transmitted.

(5) A document is made available on a web-site in accordance with this subsection if—

(a) the recipient has agreed that documents may be delivered to him by being made available on a website;

(b) the document is a document to which that agreement applies and is made available on a website;

(c) the recipient is notified, in a manner agreed by him; of—

(i)   the presence of the document on the website;
(ii) the address of the website; and
(iii) the place on the website where the document may be accessed.

(6) A document made available on a website in accordance with subsection (5) shall, unless the contrary is proved, be treated as having been delivered at 9 a.m. on the working day immediately

following the day on which the recipient is notified in accordance with subsection (5)(c).

(7) In this section—

"electronic address" includes any number or address used for the purposes of receiving electronic communications;

"electronic communication" means an electronic communication within the meaning of the Electronic Communications Act 2000 (c.7) the processing of which on receipt is intended to produce writing;

"electronic communications network" means an electronic communications network within the meaning of the Communications Act 2003 (c.21);

"electronically" means in the form of an electronic communication;

"working day" means a day which is not a Saturday or a Sunday, Christmas Day, Good Friday or a bank holiday in England and Wales under the Banking and Financial Dealings Act 1971 (c.80).

A1–50   s.81 Power to make further provision about documents in electronic form

(1) Regulations may amend section 80 by modifying the circumstances in which, and the conditions subject to which, the delivery of a document for the purposes of section 79(2)(a) may be effected by—

    (a) transmitting the document electronically; or

    (b) making the document available on a website.

(2) Regulations may also amend section 80 by modifying the day on which and the time at which documents which are transmitted electronically or made available on a website in accordance with that section are to be treated as having been delivered.

(3) Regulations under this section may make such consequential amendments of this Part as the person making the regulations considers appropriate.

(4) The power to make such regulations shall be exercisable—

    (a) in relation to documents relating to complaints about hedges situated in England, by the Secretary of State; and

(b) in relation to documents relating to complaints about hedges situated in Wales, by the National Assembly for Wales.

(5) In this section "electronically" has the meaning given in section 80.

s.82 Interpretation

In this Part—

"the appeal authority" has the meaning given by section 71(7);

"complaint" shall be construed in accordance with section 65;

"complainant" has the meaning given by section 65(5);

"the compliance period" has the meaning given by section 69(6);

"domestic property" has the meaning given by section 67;

"high hedge" has the meaning given by section 66;

"local authority", in relation to England, means—

    (a) a district council;
    (b) a county council for a county in which there are no districts;
    (c) a London borough council; or
    (d) the Common Council of the City of London;

and, in relation to Wales, means a county council or a county borough council;

"the neighbouring land" has the meaning given by section 65(5);

"occupier", in relation to any land, means a person entitled to possession of the land by virtue of an estate or interest in it;

"the operative date" shall be construed in accordance with sections 69(5) and 73(5) and (6);

"owner", in relation to any land, means a person (other than a mortgagee not in possession) who, whether in his own right or as trustee for any person—

    (a) is entitled to receive the rack rent of the land; or
    (b) where the land is not let at a rack rent, would be so entitled if it were so let;

"preventative action" has the meaning given by section 69(9);

"the relevant authority" has the meaning given by section 65(5);

"remedial notice" shall be construed in accordance with section 69(1);

"remedial action" has the meaning given by section 69(9).

A1–52   s.83 Power to amend sections 65 and 66

(1) Regulations may do one or both of the following—

  (a) amend section 65 for the purpose of extending the scope of complaints relating to high hedges to which this Part applies; and

  (b) amend section 66 (definition of "high hedge").

(2) The power to make such regulations shall be exercisable—

  (a) in relation to complaints about hedges situated in England, by the Secretary of State; and

  (b) in relation to complaints about hedges situated in Wales, by the National Assembly for Wales.

(3) Regulations under this section may make such consequential amendments of this Part as the person making the regulations considers appropriate.

A1–53   s.84 Crown application

(1) This Part and any provision made under it bind the Crown.

(2) This section does not impose criminal liability on the Crown.

(3) Subsection (2) does not affect the criminal liability of persons in the service of the Crown.

Appendix 2

Statutory Instruments

Town and Country Planning (General Permitted Development) Order 1995

S.I. 1995/418

Art.3 Permitted development

(1) Subject to the provisions of this Order and regulations 60 to 63 of the Conservation (Natural Habitats, etc.) Regulations 1994 (general development orders), planning permission is hereby granted for the classes of development described as permitted development in Schedule 2.

(2) Any permission granted by paragraph (1) is subject to any relevant exception, limitation or condition specified in Schedule 2.

Schedule 2
Schedule Part 2 Minor Operations

Para.A Permitted development

The erection, construction, maintenance, improvement or alteration of a gate, fence, wall or other means of enclosure.

Para.A1
1) Development not permitted Development is not permitted by Class A if—

(a) the height of any gate, fence, wall or means of enclosure erected or constructed adjacent to a highway used by vehicular traffic would, after the carrying out of the development, exceed one metre above ground level;

(b) the height of any other gate, fence, wall or means of enclosure erected or constructed would exceed two metres above ground level;

(c) the height of any gate, fence, wall or other means of enclosure maintained, improved or altered would, as a result of the development, exceed its former height or the height referred to in sub-paragraph (a) or (b) as the height appropriate to it if erected or constructed, whichever is the greater; or

(d) it would involve development within the curtilage of, or to a gate, fence, wall or other means of enclosure surrounding, a listed building.

Hedgerows Regulations 1997

S.I. 1997/1160

A2–03   **Reg.1 Citation and commencement**

These Regulations may be cited as the Hedgerows Regulations 1997 and shall come into force on 1st June 1997.

A2–04   **Reg.2 Interpretation**

(1) In these Regulations—

"the 1990 Act" means the Town and Country Planning Act 1990;

"the 1995 Act" means the Environment Act 1995;

"agriculture" includes horticulture, fruit growing, seed growing, dairy farming, the breeding and keeping of livestock (including any creature kept for the production of food, wool, skins or fur, or for the purposes of its use in the farming of land), the use of land as grazing land, meadow land, osier land, market gardens and nursery grounds, and the use of land for woodlands where that use is ancillary to the farming of land for other agricultural purposes, and "agricultural" shall be construed accordingly;

"agricultural holding" has the same meaning as in the Agricultural Holdings Act 1986;

"common land" has the same meaning as in the Commons Registration Act 1965, and references to common land include town or village green within the meaning of that Act;

"farm business tenancy" has the same meaning as in the Agricultural Tenancies Act 1995;

"gap", in relation to a hedgerow, means any opening (whether or not it is filled);

"hedgerow removal notice" means a notice under regulation 5(1)(a);

"hedgerow retention notice" means a notice referred to in regulation 5(2);

"local planning authority", except in paragraph 5(b)(ii) of Part II of Schedule 1, means—

(a) as regards land within a National Park, the National Park Authority for that Park;

(b) as regards land within the Broads, within the meaning of the Norfolk and Suffolk Broads Act 1988, the Broads Authority;

(c) as regards the Isles of Scilly, the Council of the Isles of Scilly;

(d) as regards any other land in England, the district planning authority within the meaning of the 1990 Act;

(e) as regards any other land in Wales, the county council or county borough council;

"notice" means notice in writing;

"owner"—

(a) in relation to a hedgerow growing on any land which comprises part of an agricultural holding or which is subject to a farm business tenancy, means the person who owns the freehold of the land or the tenant;

(b) in relation to a hedgerow growing on any other land, means the person who owns the freehold of the land;

and

"owns the freehold" means is entitled, otherwise than as a mortgagee not in possession, to dispose of the fee simple;

"protected land" means—

(a) land managed as a nature reserve in pursuance of section 21 (establishment of nature reserves by local authorities) of the National Parks and Access to the Countryside Act 1949;

(b) land in relation to which a notification under section 28 (areas of special scientific interest) of the Wildlife and Countryside Act 1981 is in force;

"relevant utility operator", in relation to any hedgerow, means—

(a) any person who holds a licence granted under section 6 of the Electricity Act 1989 (power to grant licences for the generation, transmission or supply of electricity) and who wishes to remove or, as the case may be, removes the hedgerow in question for the purpose of carrying out any activity authorised by that licence;

(b) any person who holds a licence granted or treated as granted under section 7 of the Gas Act 1986 (power to grant licences for the conveyance of gas through pipes) and who wishes to remove or, as the case may be, removes the hedgerow in question for the purpose of carrying out any activity authorised by that licence;

(c) any person who holds a licence granted under section 7 of the Telecommunications Act 1984 (power to licence telecommunications systems) which applies to him the telecommunications code contained in Schedule 2 to that Act and who wishes to remove or, as the case may be, removes the hedgerow in question in pursuance of a right conferred by the telecommunications code and in accordance with the provisions of his licence;

(d) a sewerage undertaker or a water undertaker which wishes to remove or, as the case may be, removes the hedgerow in question for the purpose of carrying out its functions, within the meaning of the Water Industry Act 1991.

(2) In these Regulations a reference to a numbered regulation or Schedule is to the regulation in, or Schedule to, these Regulations which is so numbered and a reference in a regulation or Schedule to a numbered paragraph, or in a paragraph to a numbered sub-paragraph, is to a paragraph or sub-paragraph of that regulation, Schedule or paragraph.

(3) Part I of Schedule 1 shall have effect for the purposes of interpretation of that Schedule, and Schedules 2 and 3 shall have effect for the purposes of that Part.

Reg.3 Application of Regulations

(1) Subject to paragraph (3), these Regulations apply to any hedgerow growing in, or adjacent to, any common land, protected land, or land used for agriculture, forestry or the breeding or keeping of horses, ponies or donkeys, if—

    (a) it has a continuous length of, or exceeding, 20 metres; or

    (b) it has a continuous length of less than 20 metres and, at each end, meets (whether by intersection or junction) another hedgerow.

(2) Subject to paragraph (3), a hedgerow is also one to which these Regulations apply if it is a stretch of hedgerow forming part of a hedgerow such as is described in paragraph (1).

(3) These Regulations do not apply to any hedgerow within the curtilage of, or marking a boundary of the curtilage of, a dwelling-house.

(4) A hedgerow which meets (whether by intersection or junction) another hedgerow is to be treated as ending at the point of intersection or junction.

(5) For the purposes of ascertaining the length of any hedgerow—

    (a) any gap resulting from a contravention of these Regulations; and

    (b) any gap not exceeding 20 metres;

shall be treated as part of the hedgerow.

Reg.4 Criteria for determining "important" hedgerows

For the purposes of section 97 (hedgerows) of the Environment Act 1995 and these Regulations, a hedgerow is "important" if it, or the hedgerow of which it is a stretch—

    (a) has existed for 30 years or more; and

    (b) satisfies at least one of the criteria listed in Part II of Schedule 1.

A2–07   **Reg.5 Removal of hedgerows**

(1) Subject to the exceptions specified in regulation 6, the removal of a hedgerow to which these Regulations apply is prohibited unless—

(a) the local planning authority in whose area the hedgerow is situated or, where it is situated in the area of more than one such authority, the local planning authority in whose area the greater part of the hedgerow is situated, have received from an owner of the hedgerow (subject to paragraph (10)) notice in the form set out in Schedule 4, or a form substantially to the same effect, of his proposal to remove the hedgerow ("hedgerow removal notice") together with the plan and evidence mentioned in the form set out in Schedule 4; and

(b)

(i) the authority have given to the person who gave the hedgerow removal notice written notice stating that the hedgerow may be removed; or

(ii) the period specified in paragraph (6) has expired without the authority having given to that person a hedgerow retention notice stating that the work may not be carried out; and

(c) the removal is carried out in accordance with the proposal specified in the hedgerow removal notice; and

(d) the hedgerow is removed within the period of two years beginning with the date of service of the hedgerow removal notice.

(2) A local planning authority which has received a hedgerow removal notice shall, consistently with paragraph (5) and within the period specified in paragraph (6), decide whether or not to give notice to that person stating that the work or, where the hedgerow removal notice refers to more than one hedgerow, so much of the work as may be specified by the authority in their notice, may not be carried out ("hedgerow retention notice").

(3) Where a hedgerow in respect of which the local planning authority has received a hedgerow removal notice is situated in a parish in England for which there is a parish council, or in a community in Wales for which there is a community council, that authority shall consult that council (or, where there is more than one such council, each of them) on the proposal to remove that hedgerow.

(4) The consultation referred to in paragraph (3) shall be completed before the period specified in paragraph (6) expires and before the

giving of a notice under paragraph (1)(b)(i) or a hedgerow retention notice.

(5) A local planning authority—

(a) shall not give a hedgerow retention notice in respect of a hedgerow which is not an "important" hedgerow;

(b) shall give such a notice, within the period specified in paragraph (6), in respect of an "important" hedgerow unless satisfied, having regard in particular to the reasons given for its proposed removal in the hedgerow removal notice, that there are circumstances which justify the hedgerow's removal.

(6) The period referred to in paragraphs (1)(b)(ii), (2), (4) and (5)(b) is that of 42 days beginning with the date on which the hedgerow removal notice is received by the local planning authority or such longer period as may be agreed between the person who gave the notice and the authority.

(7) A hedgerow retention notice shall, except where regulation 8(4) applies, specify each criterion (of those listed in Schedule 1) which applies to the hedgerow to which the notice relates.

(8) A hedgerow retention notice may be withdrawn at any time by the local planning authority by giving written notice of the withdrawal to the person to whom the hedgerow retention notice was given.

(9) Where a hedgerow retention notice has been given stating that work relating to a hedgerow may not be carried out, and that notice has not been withdrawn, removal of the hedgerow consisting of or including any such work is prohibited.

(10) Where a hedgerow is or is to be removed by or on behalf of a relevant utility operator from land of which it is not the owner, paragraph (1)(a) shall apply as though the reference to the owner were instead a reference to the relevant utility operator.

Reg.6 Permitted work   A2–08

(1) The removal of any hedgerow to which these Regulations apply is permitted if it is required—

(a) for making a new opening in substitution for an existing opening which gives access to land, but subject to paragraph (2);

(b) for obtaining temporary access to any land in order to give assistance in an emergency;

(c) for obtaining access to land where another means of access is not available or is available only at disproportionate cost;

(d) for the purposes of national defence;

(e) for carrying out development for which planning permission has been granted or is deemed to have been granted, except development for which permission is granted by article 3 of the Town and Country Planning General Permitted Development Order 1995 in respect of development of any of the descriptions contained in Schedule 2 to that Order other than Parts 11 (development under local or private Acts or orders) and 30 (toll road facilities);

(f) for carrying out, pursuant to, or under, the Land Drainage Act 1991, the Water Resources Act 1991 or the Environment Act 1995, work for the purpose of flood defence or land drainage;

(g) for preventing the spread of, or ensuring the eradication of—

   (i) any plant pest, within the meaning of the Plant Health (Great Britain) Order 1993, in respect of which any action is being, or is to be, taken under article 22 or 23 of that Order; or

   (ii) any tree pest, within the meaning of the Plant Health (Forestry) (Great Britain) Order 1993, in respect of which any action is being, or is to be, taken under article 21 or 22 of that Order;

(h) for the carrying out by the Secretary of State of his functions in respect of any highway for which he is the highway authority or in relation to which, by virtue of section 4(2) of the Highways Act 1980, he has the same powers under that Act as the local highway authority;

(i) for carrying out any felling, lopping or cutting back required or permitted as a consequence of any notice given or order made under paragraph 9 of Schedule 4 to the Electricity Act 1989 (felling, lopping or cutting back to prevent obstruction of or interference with electric lines and plant or to prevent danger); or

(j) for the proper management of the hedgerow.

(2) Where the removal of a hedgerow to which these Regulations apply is permitted by these Regulations only by paragraph (1)(a), the person removing it shall fill the existing opening by planting a hedge within 8 months of the making of the new opening.

(3) The fact that work is permitted under these Regulations does not affect any prohibition or restriction imposed by or under any other enactment or by any agreement.

Reg.7 Offences

(1) A person who intentionally or recklessly removes, or causes or permits another person to remove, a hedgerow in contravention of regulation 5(1) or (9) is guilty of an offence.

(2) A person who contravenes or fails to comply with regulation 6(2) is guilty of an offence.

(3) Hedgerows to which these Regulations apply are prescribed for the purposes of section 97(4)(d) of the 1995 Act (which relates to offences triable either way).

(4) A person guilty of an offence under paragraph (1) shall be liable—

    (a) on summary conviction, to a fine not exceeding the statutory maximum; or

    (b) on conviction on indictment, to a fine.

(5) A person guilty of an offence under paragraph (2) shall be liable on summary conviction to a fine not exceeding level 3 on the standard scale.

(6) In determining the amount of any fine to be imposed on a person convicted of an offence under paragraph (1) or (2), the court shall in particular have regard to any financial benefit which has accrued or appears likely to accrue to him in consequence of the offence.

(7) Section 331 (offences by corporations) of the 1990 Act shall apply in relation to offences under paragraph (1) or (2) committed by a body corporate as it applies in relation to offences under that Act committed by a body corporate.

A2–10   **Reg.8 Replacement of hedgerows**

(1) Subject to regulation 15, where it appears to the local planning authority that a hedgerow has been removed in contravention of regulation 5(1) or (9), the authority may (whether or not proceedings are instituted under regulation 7), give a notice to the owner, requiring him to plant another hedgerow or, where the hedgerow has been removed by or on behalf of a relevant utility operator, give a notice to that operator requiring it to plant another hedgerow.

(2) A notice under paragraph (1) shall specify the species and position of the shrubs, or trees and shrubs, to be planted and the period within which the planting is to be carried out.

(3) Subsections (1), (2) and (6) of section 209 (execution and cost of works required by s.207 notice) of the 1990 Act shall apply, with the necessary modifications, to shrubs and trees whose planting is required by a notice under paragraph (1) as if they were trees whose planting was required by a notice under subsection (1) of section 207 (enforcement of duties as to replacement of trees) of that Act.

(4) A hedgerow planted in compliance with a notice under paragraph (1) or by virtue of paragraph (3) shall be treated—

    (a) for the purposes of these Regulations;

    (b) for the period of 30 years beginning with the date of substantial completion of the planting;

as if it were an "important" hedgerow within the meaning of regulation 4.

A2–11   **Reg.9 Appeals**

(1) Subject to regulation 15, a person to whom a hedgerow retention notice or a notice under regulation 8(1) is given may, by notice given within 28 days from the date on which the notice was given to him, or such longer period as the Secretary of State may allow, appeal to the Secretary of State.

(2) The notice of appeal shall state the grounds for the appeal and the appellant shall serve a copy of it on the local planning authority which gave the hedgerow retention notice or notice under regulation 8(1).

(3) In determining the appeal the Secretary of State—

(a) may allow or dismiss it, either as to the whole or as to part;

(b) shall give any directions necessary to give effect to his determination, including directions for quashing or modifying any
notice;

and he shall notify the appellant and the local planning authority of
his determination of the appeal.

(4) Before determining the appeal, the Secretary of State shall afford
to the appellant and the local planning authority an opportunity, if
they so wish, of appearing before, and being heard by, a person
appointed by the Secretary of State for the purpose.

(5) The Secretary of State may cause a local inquiry to be held in
connection with an appeal and subsections (2) to (5) of section 250
of the Local Government Act 1972 (local inquiries: evidence and
costs) shall apply to any such inquiry.

(6) The Secretary of State shall have the same powers to appoint a
person to exercise functions in connection with appeals under this
regulation as he is given by section 114 of the 1995 Act in relation to
his functions specified in that section; and the provisions of Schedule 20 to that Act shall apply with respect to any such appointment
as it applies to appointments under that section.

(7) The Secretary of State and any person appointed by him for any
purpose of this regulation shall, except where the appeal is disposed
of on the basis of written representations and other documents, have
the same power to make orders under section 250(5) of the Local
Government Act 1972 (orders with respect to costs of the parties) in
relation to proceedings on an appeal under this regulation which do
not give rise to an inquiry as he has in relation to an inquiry and section 322A (orders as to costs: supplementary) of the 1990 Act shall
apply to proceedings on an appeal under this regulation as if they
were proceedings under that Act.

Reg.10 Records   A2–12

Each local planning authority shall compile and keep available for
public inspection free of charge at all reasonable hours and at a
convenient place a record containing a copy of—

(a) every hedgerow removal notice received by them;

(b) every hedgerow retention notice issued by them;

(c) every notice given by them under regulation 5(1)(b)(i);

(d) every determination notified to them under regulation 9(3).

A2–13   Reg.11 Injunctions

(1) Where a local planning authority consider it necessary or expedient for an actual or apprehended offence under these Regulations to be restrained by injunction, they may apply to the court for an injunction, whether or not they have exercised or are proposing to exercise any of their other powers under these Regulations.

(2) On an application under paragraph (1) the court may grant such an injunction as the court thinks appropriate for the purpose of restraining the offence.

(3) In this regulation "the court" means the High Court or the county court.

A2–14   Reg.12 Rights to enter without a warrant

(1) Any person duly authorised in writing by a local planning authority may enter any land for the purpose of—

   (a) surveying it in connection with any hedgerow removal notice received by the authority;

   (b) ascertaining whether an offence under regulation 7 has been committed;

   (c) determining whether a notice should be given under regulation 8;

if there are reasonable grounds for entering for the purpose in question.

(2) Any person duly authorised in writing by the Secretary of State may enter any land for the purpose of surveying it in connection with any appeal made under regulation 9, if there are reasonable grounds for entering for that purpose.

(3) Any right to enter by virtue of paragraph (1) or (2) shall be exercised at a reasonable hour.

(4) No right to enter by virtue of paragraph (1)(a) or (2) shall be exercised in relation to land which—

(a) adjoins that in respect of which a hedgerow removal notice has been given or an appeal made; and

(b) is occupied by a person other than the person who gave the hedgerow removal notice or made the appeal;

unless at least 24 hours' notice of the intended entry has been given to the occupier of that adjoining land.

(5) In a case to which regulation 5(10) applies, no right to enter any land by virtue of paragraph (1)(a) or (2) shall be exercised unless at least 24 hours' notice of the intended entry has been given to the occupier of the land.

Reg.13 Right to enter under warrant   A2–15

(1) If it is shown to the satisfaction of a justice of the peace on sworn information in writing—

(a) that there are reasonable grounds for entering any land for any of the purposes mentioned in regulation 12(1) or (2); and

(b) that—

    (i) admission to the land has been refused, or a refusal is reasonably apprehended; or

    (ii) the case is one of urgency;

the justice may issue a warrant authorising any person duly authorised in writing by a local planning authority or, as the case may be, the Secretary of State to enter the land.

(2) For the purposes of paragraph (1)(b)(i) admission to land shall be regarded as having been refused if no reply is received to a request for admission within a reasonable period.

(3) A warrant authorises entry on one occasion only and that entry must be—

(a) within one month from the date of the issue of the warrant; and

(b) at a reasonable hour, unless the case is one of urgency.

A2–16 **Reg.14 Rights of entry: supplementary provisions**

(1) Any power conferred by virtue of regulation 12 or 13 to enter land ("a right of entry") shall be construed as including power to take samples from any hedgerow on the land and samples of the soil.

(2) A person authorised to enter land in the exercise of a right of entry—

(a) shall, if so required, produce evidence of his authority and state the purpose of his entry before so entering;

(b) may take with him such other persons as may be necessary; and

(c) on leaving the land shall, if the occupier is not then present, leave it as effectively secured against trespassers as he found it.

(3) Any person who wilfully obstructs a person acting in the exercise of a right of entry shall be guilty of an offence and liable on summary conviction to a fine not exceeding level 3 on the standard scale.

(4) If any damage is caused to land or chattels in the exercise of a right of entry, compensation may be recovered by any person suffering the damage from the authority who gave the written authority for the entry or, as the case may be, the Secretary of State.

(5) Any question of disputed compensation under this regulation shall be referred to and determined by the Lands Tribunal.

(6) In relation to the determination of any such question, the provisions of sections 2 and 4 of the Land Compensation Act 1961 shall apply subject to any necessary modifications.

A2–17 **Reg.15 Local planning authorities as owners of hedgerows**

(1) This regulation applies where a local planning authority are the owners (whether alone or jointly with others) of a hedgerow to which these Regulations apply.

(2) Notwithstanding anything in section 101 (arrangements for the discharge of functions by local authorities) of the Local Government Act 1972, a hedgerow removal notice given in a case to which this regulation applies may not be considered—

(a) by a committee or sub-committee of the authority concerned if that committee or sub-committee is responsible (wholly or partly) for the management of the land in which is situated the hedgerow to which the notice relates; or

(b) by an officer of the authority concerned if his responsibilities include any aspect of the management of the land in which is situated the hedgerow to which the notice relates.

(3) Regulations 8 and 9 do not apply in a case to which this regulation applies.

Reg.16 Application of other provisions of the 1990 Act

A2–17.1

(1) Subsections (1), (3) and (6) of section 318 (ecclesiastical property) of the 1990 Act shall apply—

(a) to notices required to be served under these Regulations on an owner of land as if those notices were notices required to be served on an owner of land under a provision of the 1990 Act; and

(b) to compensation payable under regulation 14 of these Regulations as if that compensation were compensation payable under Part IV of the 1990 Act.

(2) Subsections (1), (2) and (4) of section 329 (service of notices) of the 1990 Act shall apply to notices under these Regulations as if those notices were notices required or authorised to be given or served under that Act.

Schedule 1 Additional Criteria for Determining "Important" Hedgerows Schedule
Part I Interpretation

Para.1

A2–18

In this Schedule—

"building" includes structure;

"Record Office" means—

(a) a place appointed under section 4 of the Public Records Act 1958 (place of deposit of public records);

(b) a place at which documents are held pursuant to a transfer under section 144A(4) of the Law of Property Act 1922 or under section 36(2) of the Tithe Act 1936, including each of those provisions as applied by section 7(1) of the Local Government (Records) Act 1962; or

(c) a place at which documents are made available for inspection by a local authority pursuant to section 1 of the Local Government (Records) Act 1962;

"relevant date" means the date on which these Regulations are made;

"Sites and Monuments Record" means a record of archaeological features and sites adopted—

(a) by resolution of a local authority within the meaning of the Local Government Act 1972, or
(b) in Greater London, by the Historic Buildings and Monuments Commission;

"standard tree"—

(a) in the case of a multi-stemmed tree, means a tree which, when measured at a point 1.3 metres from natural ground level, has at least two stems whose diameters are at least 15 centimetres;
(b) in the case of a single-stemmed tree, means a tree which, when measured at a point 1.3 metres from natural ground level, has a stem whose diameter is at least 20 centimetres;

"woodland species" means the species listed in Schedule 2; and

"woody species" means the species and sub-species listed in Schedule 3, and any hybrid, that is to say, any individual plant resulting from a cross between parents of any species or sub-species so listed, but does not include any cultivar; and

references to the documents in paragraph 6(3)(b) and (4) are to those documents as at the relevant date, without taking account of any subsequent revisions, supplements or modifications.

Part II
Criteria Archaeology and History

A2–19   **Para.1**

The hedgerow marks the boundary, or part of the boundary, of at least one historic parish or township; and for this purpose "historic" means existing before 1850.

Para.2

A2–20

The hedgerow incorporates an archaeological feature which is—

    (a) included in the schedule of monuments compiled by the Secretary of State under section 1 (Schedule of monuments) of the Ancient Monuments and Archaeological Areas Act 1979; or

    (b) recorded at the relevant date in a Sites and Monuments Record.

Para.3

A2–21

The hedgerow—

    (a) is situated wholly or partly within an archaeological site included or recorded as mentioned in paragraph 2 or on land adjacent to and associated with such a site; and

    (b) is associated with any monument or feature on that site.

Para.4

A2–22

The hedgerow—

    (a) marks the boundary of a pre-1600 AD estate or manor recorded at the relevant date in a Sites and Monuments Record or in a document held at that date at a Record Office; or

    (b) is visibly related to any building or other feature of such an estate or manor.

Para.5

A2–23

The hedgerow—

    (a) is recorded in a document held at the relevant date at a Record Office as an integral part of a field system pre-dating the Inclosure Acts; or

    (b) is part of, or visibly related to, any building or other feature associated with such a system, and that system—

(i)   is substantially complete; or
(ii) is of a pattern which is recorded in a document prepared before the relevant date by a local planning authority, within the meaning of the 1990 Act, for the purposes of development control within the authority's area, as a key landscape characteristic.

A2–24   Para.6

The hedgerow—

(a) contains species listed or categorised as mentioned in sub-paragraph (3); or

(b) is referred to in a record held immediately before the relevant date by a biological record centre maintained by, or on behalf of, a local authority within the meaning of the Local Government Act 1972, and in a form recognised by the Nature Conservancy Council for England, the Countryside Council for Wales or the Joint Nature Conservation Committee, as having contained any such species—

(i)   in the case of animals and birds, subject to sub-paragraph (2), within the period of five years immediately before the relevant date;
(ii) in the case of plants, subject to sub-paragraph (2), within the period of ten years immediately before the relevant date;

(2) Where more than one record referable to the period of five or, as the case may be, ten years before the relevant date is held by a particular biological record centre, and the more (or most) recent record does not satisfy the criterion specified in sub-paragraph (1)(b), the criterion is not satisfied (notwithstanding that an earlier record satisfies it).

(3) The species referred to in sub-paragraph (1) are those—

(a) listed in Part I (protection at all times) of Schedule 1 (birds which are protected by special penalties), Schedule 5 (animals which are protected) or Schedule 8 (plants which are protected) to the Wildlife and Countryside Act 1981;

(b) categorised as a declining breeder (category 3) in "Red Data Birds in Britain" Batten L.A., Bibby C.J., Clement P., Elliott G.D. and Porter R.F. (Eds), published in 1990 for the Nature

Conservancy Council and the Royal Society for the Protection of Birds (ISBN 0 85661 056 9); or

(c) categorised as "endangered", "extinct", "rare" or "vulnerable" in Britain in a document mentioned in sub-paragraph (4).

(4) The documents referred to in sub-paragraph (3)(c) are—

(a) of the books known as the British Red Data Books:

1. "Vascular Plants" Perring F.H. and Farrell L., 2nd Edition, published in 1983 for the Royal Society for Nature Conservation (ISBN 0 902484 04 4);
2. "Insects" Shirt D.B. (Ed.), published in 1987 for the Nature Conservancy Council (ISBN 0 86139 380 5); and
3. "Invertebrates other than insects" Bratton J.H. (Ed.), published in 1991 for the Joint Nature Conservation Committee (ISBN 1 873701 00 4); and

(b) of the books known as the Red Data Books of Britain and Ireland:

"Stoneworts" Stewart N.F. and Church J.M., published in 1992 for the Joint Nature Conservation Committee (ISBN 1 873701 24 1).

Para.7

A2–25

(1) Subject to sub-paragraph (2), the hedgerow includes—

(a) at least 7 woody species;

(b) at least 6 woody species, and has associated with it at least 3 of the features specified in sub-paragraph (4);

(c) at least 6 woody species, including one of the following—

black-poplar tree (Populus nigra ssp betulifolia);
large-leaved lime (Tilia platyphyllos);
small-leaved lime (Tilia cordata);
wild service-tree (Sorbus torminalis); or

(d) at least 5 woody species, and has associated with it at least 4 of the features specified in sub-paragraph (4);

and the number of woody species in a hedgerow shall be ascertained in accordance with sub-paragraph (3).

(2) Where the hedgerow in question is situated wholly or partly in the county (as constituted on 1st April 1997) of the City of Kingston-upon-Hull, Cumbria, Darlington, Durham, East Riding of Yorkshire, Hartlepool, Lancashire, Middlesbrough, North East Lincolnshire, North Lincolnshire, Northumberland, North Yorkshire, Redcar and Cleveland, Stockton-on-Tees, Tyne and Wear, West Yorkshire or York, the number of woody species mentioned in paragraphs (a) to (d) of sub-paragraph (1) is to be treated as reduced by one.

(3) For the purposes of sub-paragraph (1) (and those of paragraph 8(b))—

   (a) where the length of the hedgerow does not exceed 30 metres, count the number of woody species present in the hedgerow;

   (b) where the length of the hedgerow exceeds 30 metres, but does not exceed 100 metres, count the number of woody species present in the central stretch of 30 metres;

   (c) where the length of the hedgerow exceeds 100 metres, but does not exceed 200 metres, count the number of woody species present in the central stretch of 30 metres within each half of the hedgerow and divide the aggregate by two;

   (d) where the length of the hedgerow exceeds 200 metres, count the number of woody species present in the central stretch of 30 metres within each third of the hedgerow and divide the aggregate by three.

(4) The features referred to in sub-paragraph (1)(b) and (d) (which include those referred to in paragraph 8(b)) are—

   (a) a bank or wall which supports the hedgerow along at least one half of its length;

   (b) gaps which in aggregate do not exceed 10% of the length of the hedgerow;

   (c) where the length of the hedgerow does not exceed 50 metres, at least one standard tree;

   (d) where the length of the hedgerow exceeds 50 metres but does not exceed 100 metres, at least 2 standard trees;

   (e) where the length of the hedgerow exceeds 100 metres, such number of standard trees (within any part of its length) as would when averaged over its total length amount to at least one for each 50 metres;

(f)   at least 3 woodland species within one metre, in any direction, of the outermost edges of the hedgerow;

(g)   a ditch along at least one half of the length of the hedgerow;

(h)   connections scoring 4 points or more in accordance with sub-paragraph (5);

(i)   a parallel hedge within 15 metres of the hedgerow.

(5) For the purposes of sub-paragraph (4)(h) a connection with another hedgerow scores one point and a connection with a pond or a woodland in which the majority of trees are broad-leaved trees scores 2 points; and a hedgerow is connected with something not only if it meets it but also if it has a point within 10 metres of it and would meet it if the line of the hedgerow continued.

Para.8   A2–26

The hedgerow—

(a)   is adjacent to a bridleway or footpath, within the meaning of the Highways Act 1980, a road used as a public path, within the meaning of section 54 (duty to reclassify roads used as public paths) of the Wildlife and Countryside Act 1981, or a byway open to all traffic, within the meaning of Part III of the Wildlife and Countryside Act 1981, and

(b)   includes at least 4 woody species, ascertained in accordance with paragraph 7(3) and at least 2 of the features specified in paragraph 7(4)(a) to (g).

Schedule 2 Woodland Species

[Species listed.]   A2–27

Schedule 3 Woody Species

[Species listed.]   A2–28

A2–29   **Schedule 4**

Form of Hedgerow Removal Notice

The Environment Act 1995

The Hedgerows Regulations 1997

To: *(Name and address of local planning authority)* ....
....
....

From: *(Name and address of person giving the notice)* ....
....
....

    1. I give you notice under regulation 5(1)(a) of the above Regulations that I propose to remove the [stretch(es) of] hedgerow(s) indicated on the attached plan. *(If possible, please provide a plan to a scale of 1:2500. A different scale can be used so long as it shows clearly the location and length of the hedgerow or hedgerows that you wish to remove.)*

    2. The reasons why I propose to remove it/them are the following:—

    3. Of the [stretch(es) of] hedgerow(s) indicated, those marked with an "X" were planted less than 30 years ago. Evidence of the date of planting is attached.

    4. I am/We are the owner(s) of the freehold of the land concerned.

    OR (please delete as appropriate)
    I am/We are the tenant(s) of the agricultural holding concerned.

    OR (please delete as appropriate)
    I am/We are the tenant(s) under the farm business tenancy concerned

    OR (please delete as appropriate)
    I am/act for the utility operator concerned.

....
(Signature of person giving notice)   *(Date)*

Land Registration Rules 2003
Part 10 Boundaries

S.I. 2003/1417

r.117 Definition

A2–30

In this Part, except in rule 121, "boundary" includes part only of a boundary.

r.118 Application for the determination of the exact line of a boundary

A2–31

(1) A proprietor of a registered estate may apply to the registrar for the exact line of the boundary of that registered estate to be determined.

(2) An application under paragraph (1) must be made in Form DB and be accompanied by—

    (a) a plan, or a plan and a verbal description, identifying the exact line of the boundary claimed and showing sufficient surrounding physical features to allow the general position of the boundary to be drawn on the Ordnance Survey map; and

    (b) evidence to establish the exact line of the boundary.

r.119 Procedure on an application for the determination of the exact line of a boundary

A2–32

(1) Where the registrar is satisfied that—

    (a) the plan, or plan and verbal description, supplied in accordance with rule 118(2)(a) identifies the exact line of the boundary claimed;

    (b) the applicant has shown an arguable case that the exact line of the boundary is in the position shown on the plan, or plan and verbal description, supplied in accordance with rule 118(2)(a); and

    (c) he can identify all the owners of the land adjoining the boundary to be determined and has an address at which each owner may be given notice;

he must give the owners of the land adjoining the boundary to be determined (except the applicant) notice of the application to determine the exact line of the boundary and of the effect of paragraph (6).

(2) Where the evidence supplied in accordance with rule 118(2)(b) includes an agreement in writing as to the exact line of the boundary with an owner of the land adjoining the boundary, the registrar need not give notice of the application to that owner.

(3) Subject to paragraph (4), the time fixed by the notice to the owner of the land to object to the application shall be the period ending at 12 noon on the twentieth business day after the date of issue of the notice or such longer period as the registrar may decide before the issue of the notice.

(4) The period set for the notice under paragraph (3) may be extended for a particular recipient of the notice by the registrar following a request by that recipient, received by the registrar before that period has expired, setting out why an extension should be allowed.

(5) If a request is received under paragraph (4) the registrar may, if he considers it appropriate, seek the views of the applicant and if, after considering any such views and all other relevant matters, he is satisfied that a longer period should be allowed he may allow such period as he considers appropriate, whether or not the period is the same as any period requested by the recipient of the notice.

(6) Unless any recipient of the notice objects to the application to determine the exact line of the boundary within the time fixed by the notice (as extended under paragraph (5), if applicable), the registrar must complete the application.

(7) Where the registrar is not satisfied as to paragraph (1)(a), (b) and (c), he must cancel the application.

(8) In this rule, the "owner of the land" means—

(a) a person entitled to apply to be registered as the proprietor of an unregistered legal estate in land under section 3 of the Act;

(b) the proprietor of any registered estate or charge affecting the land; and

(c) if the land is demesne land, Her Majesty.

r.120 Completion of application for the exact line of a boundary to be determined

(1) Where the registrar completes an application under rule 118, he must—

    (a) make an entry in the individual register of the applicant's registered title and, if appropriate, in the individual register of any superior or inferior registered title, and any registered title affecting the other land adjoining the determined boundary, stating that the exact line of the boundary is determined under section 60 of the Act; and

    (b) subject to paragraph (2), add to the title plan of the applicant's registered title and, if appropriate, to the title plan of any superior or inferior registered title, and any registered title affecting the other land adjoining the determined boundary, such particulars of the exact line of the boundary as he considers appropriate.

(2) Instead of, or as well as, adding particulars of the exact line of the boundary to the title plans mentioned in paragraph (1)(b), the registrar may make an entry in the individual registers mentioned in paragraph (1)(a) referring to any other plan showing the exact line of the boundary.

r.121 Relationship between determined and undetermined parts of a boundary

Where the exact line of part of the boundary of a registered estate has been determined, the ends of that part of the boundary are not to be treated as determined for the purposes of adjoining parts of the boundary the exact line of which has not been determined.

r.122 Determination of the exact line of a boundary without application

(1) This rule applies where—

    (a) there is—

        (i) a transfer of part of a registered estate in land; or

        (ii) the grant of a term of years absolute which is a registrable disposition of part of a registered estate in land;

(b) there is a common boundary; and

(c) there is sufficient information in the disposition to enable the registrar to determine the exact line of the common boundary.

(2) The registrar may determine the exact line of the common boundary and if he does he must—

(a) make an entry in the individual registers of the affected registered titles stating that the exact line of the common boundary is determined under section 60 of the Act; and

(b) subject to paragraph (3), add to the title plan of the disponor's affected registered title (whether or not the disponor is still the proprietor of that title, or still entitled to be registered as proprietor of that title) and to the title plan of the registered title under which the disposition is being registered, such particulars of the exact line of the common boundary as he considers appropriate.

(3) Instead of, or as well as, adding particulars of the exact line of the common boundary to the title plans mentioned in paragraph (2)(b), the registrar may make an entry in the individual registers of the affected registered titles referring to the description of the common boundary in the disposition.

(4) In this rule—

"common boundary" means any boundary of the land disposed of by a disposition which adjoins land in which the disponor at the date of the disposition had a registered estate in land or of which such disponor was entitled to be registered as proprietor, and

"disposition" means a transfer or grant mentioned in paragraph (1)(a).

A2–36   r.123 Agreement about accretion or diluvion

(1) An application to register an agreement about the operation of accretion or diluvion in relation to a registered estate in land must be made by, or be accompanied by the consent of, the proprietor of the registered estate and of any registered charge, except that no such consent is required from a person who is party to the agreement.

(2) On registration of such an agreement the registrar must make a note in the property register that the agreement is registered for the purposes of section 61(2) of the Act.

Index

waste land, 1–32
registered land, 1–40—1–42
  application to Registry, 1–41
  determined boundaries,
    1–41
  general boundaries, 1–40
  registered boundary
    agreement, 1–42
  variation. *See* Variation of
    boundaries
Ditches, 1–16
Duchy of Cornwall lands
  boundary disputes, 3–23
Duty to fence, 6–01—6–26
  animals, 6–19
  burial grounds, 6–23
  churchyards, 6–23
  commonhold units, 6–06
  commons, 6–27
  covenants not to fence, 6–26
  covenants on conveying
    freeholds, 6–02—6–04
    lease at peppercorn rent,
      6–04
    methods of attaching fencing
      obligation, 6–02
    rentcharge, and, 6–02, 6–03
    right of re-entry, 6–03
  damage, liability for, 6–01
  damages on breach of
    covenant, 6–06
  dangerous objects and
    operations, 6–20
    negligence, 6–20
    occupiers' liability, 6–20
    Rylands v Fletcher, 6–20
  disused mines, 6–24
  fencing easements, 6–12, 6–13.
    See also Fencing easements
  highway and land adjoining,
    6–14—6–20
    animals, 6–14
    barbed wire, 6–15
    cellars, 6–16
    dilapidation, 6–14
    duty of highway authority to
      fence, 6–16

    fence or hedge in highway,
      6–16
    opening outwards, 6–15
    overhanging hedge, tree or
      shrub, 6–15
    source of danger, 6–14
  land accessible to public, 6–17
  land adjoining common, 6–18
  landlord and tenant,
    6–07—6–11
    agricultural holdings, 6–08
    benefits and burdens of
      covenants, 6–07
    compensation, 6–11
    covenants implied at
      common law, 6–10
    enforcement of covenant,
      6–07
    estovers, 6–10
    express covenants, 6–07
    implied obligations, 6–07
    short residential lettings,
      6–09
  local legislation, 6–25
  no general duty, 6–01
  obligation not to fence, 6–26
  obligations on freehold owners,
    6–02—6–06
  parsonages, 6–22
  railways, 6–21
  statutory obligations,
    6–21—6–25

Ecclesiastical terriers
  evidence, as, 3–11
Estoppel
  variation of boundaries, and,
    1–46
Estovers, 6–10

Fencing easements, 6–12, 6–13
  evidence, 6–12
  liability, 6–13
  penetration of weather, 6–13
  title to right, 6–12
Flats, 1–13
  horizontal boundaries, 1–38